Get **more** out of libraries

Please return or renew this item by the last date shown.
You can renew online at www.hants.gov.uk/library
Or by phoning 0845 603 5631

Hampshire
County Council

Dark
is the
Dawn

**The story of an ordinary family
in extraordinary times**

Cynthia Morey

In memory of my brother Paul
and the boys of Bomber Command

Published by Cynthia Morey
Publishing partner: Paragon Publishing, Rothersthorpe
First published 2009
© Cynthia Morey 2009

Cover photo: A Wellington Mk 11 being prepared for a night operation in February 1942 from which it did not return. (Gerry Tyack Collection)

ISBN 978-1-899820-61-0
Book design, layout and production management by Into Print
www.intoprint.net
Printed and bound in UK and USA by Lightning Source

ACKNOWLEDGMENTS

I am indebted to my friend Janet Leonard (Cambray) for her invaluable help in remembering all the things we got up to at Leamington College for Girls during those war years. It was such fun delving into the past and I am appreciative of her prodigious memory.

I also wish to thank Gerry V Tyack, of the Wellington Aviation Museum, Moreton-in-Marsh, for the stunning cover photograph.

Thanks also to Alan Brodie Representation Ltd for permission to include Noël Coward's evocative poem 'Lie in the Dark and Listen'.

Above all, I am grateful to my husband Anthony Jennings for his unfailing encouragement and support for my writing. I must try his patience at times, but he never shows it!

LIE IN THE DARK AND LISTEN

Lie in the dark and listen.
It's clear tonight so they're flying high,
Hundreds of them, thousands perhaps,
Riding the icy moonlit sky.
Men, machinery, bombs and maps,
Altimeters, guns and charts,
Coffee, sandwiches, fleece-lined boots,
Bones and muscles and minds and hearts.
English saplings with English roots
Deep in the earth they've left below.
Lie in the dark and let them go,
Lie in the dark and listen.

Lie in the dark and listen.
They're going over in waves and waves
High above villages, hills and streams,
Country churches and little graves
And little citizens' worried dreams;
Very soon they'll have reached the sea
And far beneath them will lie the bays
And cliffs and sands where they used to be
Taken for summer holidays.
Lie in the dark and let them go,
Theirs is a world we'll never know.
Lie in the dark and listen.

Lie in the dark and listen.
City magnates and steel contractors,
Factory workers and politicians,
Soft hysterical little actors,
Ballet dancers, reserved musicians
Safe in your warm civilian beds,
Count your profits and count your sheep,
Life is passing above your heads.
Just turn over and try to sleep.
Lie in the dark and let them go,
There's one debt you'll forever owe.
Lie in the dark and listen.

NOEL COWARD

Written in tribute to Bomber Command 1943
by permission of Alan Brodie Representation Ltd,
abr@alanbrodie.com

FOREWORD

This story, though inevitably based on my own personal experience, is intended to represent that of any ordinary family who lived through those tranquil pre-war years before being plunged into the devastating times that followed. We were not special in any way – neither rich nor poor – three children living with their parents in a terraced house in Portsmouth, leading the sort of lives that so many did. It has, of necessity, to be a sort of autobiography, but it's written on behalf of everyone who lived through the events that we did.

When I began this account of my childhood I wondered how much detail I might be able to recall. I needn't have worried – it was all there, stacked away in my memory, and came tumbling out faster than I could commit it to paper. Even memories of the carefree pre-war period when I was very young came rushing back – things I thought I had forgotten re-emerged in detail and flashed across my mind with startling clarity. Book after book of old black and white 'snaps', taken with a Kodak 'Brownie' box camera, sparked off even more recollections of summer holidays, picnics, excursions or just everyday happenings, and a pile of ancient, dog-eared school exercise books brought back vivid memories of school days. I make no apology for including a few excerpts from these; those grubby pages set the period so well and illustrate graphically the sort of education we received then – both prior to the war and during those troubled years. There was even a 1939 diary written in a round childish hand which re-created the atmosphere of those times. I was both amused and astonished at the way we lived then – the simple, unsophisticated lives we led, the discipline we took for granted, yet the freedom we enjoyed and the modest demands we made of life. What an extraordinary change in lifestyle has occurred since I was a child. Has it all been the effect of the Second World War? How different might life be now if it had not occurred? We shall never know.

We were just an ordinary family, neither rich nor poor. We saved up hard for anything we wanted – sometimes for a long time – but what an achievement it was when at last we had enough money to buy the object of our desire, and how we valued it. Holidays were basic, simple and local, but no less enjoyable for that. Scholarships had to be won in order to progress to higher education – little money was available for private tuition. Many of our clothes were made at home, on a hand-operated sewing machine. There was no attitude that the world owed us a living – we understood that people like us worked and waited for the good things in life. That was the way an ordinary family like ours in the nineteen-thirties lived, and uneventful and uncomplicated though it was, we were happy with it.

Though the Second World War, with its terror and tragedies overshadowed my most impressionable years, I have a sneaking feeling that in a strange way I am not altogether sorry to have lived through it. Those were extraordinary times and I am glad that I experienced the wonderful comradeship and fortitude of the British people under such relentless pressure and hardship. There was a togetherness which is hard to imagine now. We had enormous pride in our country then – a pride that hardly exists today, submerged as we are in a sea of foolish political correctness.

There are countless books, broadcasts, television plays and documentaries nowadays about World War II – more seem to appear every day – and they never fail to attract my interest. Often I say, 'Yes – I remember *that*' or 'Goodness – I'd forgotten all about *that*', but sometimes mistakes are made which cause me to remark, 'How ridiculous – it just wasn't like that at all' or 'We didn't speak like that then – we didn't use those expressions'. So I'm trying in this book to put myself firmly back in those times, avoid anachronisms and depict life as it really was in those never to be forgotten years. I hope, in some small measure, that I've succeeded.

I make no excuse for the fact that as a young teenager I was completely besotted with the RAF, its aircraft, and the men who flew in them, for my beloved brother was one of their number. I studied every book on aircraft I could get hold of, knew all there was to know about cowlings and engines and ailerons, drew and painted Spitfires, Hurricanes, Wellingtons and Blenheims, and composed rather awful poems about them. Nearly every essay I ever wrote at school ended up involving the RAF, however remote the original subject! I still have an enormous interest in World War II aircraft, and a sighting of the RAF Memorial Flight can send me into ecstasies. The sound of those six Merlin engines is almost more than I can bear. It is such a pity that there is no airworthy example of the Vickers Armstrong Wellington (on which my brother was a navigator-bomb aimer) as these twin-engined aircraft were the backbone of Bomber Command during the early years of the war, before the legendary Lancaster came on to the scene. Over 11,000 Wellingtons were operational in every field of war, but their only complete memorial is one solitary machine in the RAF Museum in Hendon. I find that very sad.

We are fortunate in where we live now, for we are not far from RAF Benson, also Abingdon and Fairford, where big air shows take place annually, so it is not unusual to see the odd World War II aircraft fly over. On rare and very special occasions we see the Memorial Flight on its way to a flypast. Anything like this causes us enormous excitement and much shouting, for my husband is as keen as I am on such things. He grew up during the war in Filton, opposite the Bristol aircraft factory, and as a small boy watched enthralled as the newly built Blenheims were towed down to Patchway to have their engines fitted. He, too, experienced serious air raids and tells me that when he walked to school in the morning after a night of bombing, stepping over débris and shrapnel, some of which was still warm – he always hoped that when he turned the corner, the school would have been flattened! It never was.

To our great delight, the nostalgic sound of the Merlin engine has become increasingly familiar of recent years, as Peter Vacher, who lives in a neighbouring village, has successfully rescued from dereliction, and restored, a Mark I Hurricane – and moreover, one that actually took part in the Battle of Britain – I probably saw it in action! It recently gave a flying display at the village fête, and our delight knew no bounds. When it becomes airborne we can see it from the bottom of our garden, and we watch spellbound.

So many decades have elapsed since the war, filled with momentous happenings, tragedies and great events, yet the effect of those chaotic years from 1939 to 1945 continue to influence my life. They were of course my most formative years, lasting through childhood and adolescence to young womanhood. No matter that I can pop up the road and buy anything I need nowadays – if the store cupboard is not well-stocked, I am uneasy. I find it extremely difficult to waste any food – that, at least, must be a good legacy, maybe from those far-off days of scarcity and rationing. Trying to clear out cupboards is a well nigh impossible task. 'There's a jumble sale on Saturday – I'll throw out a lot of stuff!' I say enthusiastically, throwing open wardrobe doors and delving inside. The mood soon changes. 'This might come in useful,' I say, putting back some old coat or sweater. It doesn't, of course. It never would, in a hundred years. But back it goes, the wardrobe door is closed, and off I go to to indulge in some other occupation, jumble sale forgotten. Can those 'make-do-and-mend' days still exist in my subconscious mind?

Life in wartime had its lighter moments, even in the air raid shelter. You can't be serious all the time, especially when you're young, and we *did* laugh – a lot – at the long queues for the most unlikely commodities, the people we met in the shelter, the comical 'get-ups' hastily donned for the nightly air raids, the funny situations Bombs might be falling, guns blasting, but in the midst of all this, the great British sense of humour was alive and well. Laughter and tears co-existed in equal measure. I hope I've managed to convey a little of each in this story

(And the title? I chose it on behalf of all my friends in the Gilbert and Sullivan Society, of which I have the honour to be President. They will know immediately that it's a quote from *Iolanthe* – or nearly! I think it conveys the atmosphere of those years perfectly.)

Dark
is the
Dawn

THE PRE-WAR YEARS

'The bell in the police box has gone!' I shouted up the stairs to my mother in the bathroom. 'What – *again?* Oh, bother!' was her exasperated reply (she probably muttered something much stronger under her breath) as she crossly let out the regulation five inches of water she had just run into the bath. 'I was just getting into the bath – I'll be right down!' There was a police box just along the road from us, and beside it a tall pole bearing an air raid siren. As soon as the bell rang twice we knew the siren would sound the warning, then we'd take to our heels for the shelter aross the road. It was August 1940, we were in Croydon, and air raids were frequent. We found it was almost impossible to get on with any sort of normal life, and taking a bath was always a gamble. Still, we managed, and morale was high. But I'm getting ahead of myself. To appreciate fully the catastrophic effect the Second World War had upon ordinary families such as ours we really have to experience the feeling of the tranquil everyday life of the pre-war years.

We were a family of five. My father worked for for the Post Office, which he was to do for the rest of his life, even in the army postal service during the first world war. He lived and breathed postal matters, progressing from office boy to Head Postmaster, and installing the first post office at the embryonic Heathrow Airport in the late 1940s. How he and my mother ever got together, I shall never know, for two people more different in temperament and interests I cannot imagine. They were, sadly, to drift apart in later years, though our welfare and happiness were never in question. My mother came from a prosperous family in the Isle of Wight, for my grandfather was a shipping agent in Cowes, dealing with the import and export of goods and owned several ships. He had a flourishing business, and was on friendly terms with 'Tommy' Lipton (of Lipton's Tea). The family lived in Montague House, West Cowes, which overlooked the Solent. Alas for my grandmother, her husband was rather too fond of the ladies, which eventually led to her leaving him (after ten children) for a fairly penurious life across the water in Portsmouth. There did not seem to be any suggestion of divorce proceedings – such things were relatively rare in those days I suppose, and viewed as a disgrace. I know nothing about how my grandmother made ends meet, but my mother went with her to Portsmouth and, I suppose, to earn some money was soon playing the piano, singing and dancing in a concert party, which suited her admirably. Perhaps it was after one of her shows that she and my father got together – it was never spoken of and I shall never know. She was laughing and fun-loving, and it must have been a shock to find herself married to my rather staid father and burdened with three children and the dreary domestic chores of those times. I never heard how they met or any details of the wedding – these things were never mentioned, neither are there any photographs of the event. It happened during the first world war, and that's all I know. My brother Paul was born in 1919, sister Olga in 1921, and I followed on six years later in 1927.

In a way, my family was divided in two. My mother, Paul and I somehow had a closeness which was hard to explain, for I was eight years Paul's junior. Yet he was everything to me from a very young age and it seemed that he never minded his small sister following him about with such adoration. We three had much in common – looks, colouring and general sense of humour. In the same way, my father and Olga had were similar in appearance and interests; she spent all her working life in a government office, as did he. But I don't mean to suggest that any favouritism was shown to any of us – that was not the case at all.

We lived at number twenty-three Park Crescent, Milton, Portsmouth – a terraced Edwardian house in a pleasant road close to Milton Park. A prim privet hedge screened it from the pavement. The house was one of those with an elaborately tiled path to the front door, and the name 'Normanhurst' in the glass above. Those anonymous names always amuse me – I believe Mrs Jane's house next door was called 'Ivydene'. We had a very pretty front room – known as the 'drawing room' – and used for parties, Christmases and special occasions. It had a lilac sofa, lilac and pink striped curtains, and a black carpet patterned with lilac and pink flowers. That may sound a little strange these days, but we thought it very fine. A verandah leading from the kitchen accommodated my small swing and opened on to the garden – modest in size, with a well-used lawn and large buddleia tree. No ordinary houses had central heating then of course – just open fires, and we had a fearsome geyser in the bathroom which belched forth boiling water in an uneven stream.

On the corner of the road were a few shops, and naturally the ones I remember are Arnold's the sweet shop and Smith & Vosper the bakers – oh, those cakes! Three-cornered jam puffs, Nelson cakes, doughnuts bursting with jam, Banbury cakes, and many more. In the sweet shop we would stand with bated breath as Mr Arnold weighed out two ounces of pear drops, acid drops or bullseyes with meticulous care. He would take a square of newspaper – (yes, *newspaper!*) and with a flick of the wrist, twist it into a neat cone, then fill it with the sweets he had weighed out in the shining brass scales. Or sometimes we would choose one of those long strips of Sharp's toffee in its dark blue and red wrapper, or a bar of Nestles milk chocolate – that was a special treat.

Olga was a very good dancer when she was tiny, and soon became the smallest member of 'The Dainty Dots', a group run by her dancing school. She appeared at concerts in a diminutive white suit, peaked cap and cane, singing 'When My Sugar Walks Down the Street' in a piping voice, apparently to great applause, so I heard. Paul had not shown any particular musical talent by then, apart from a certain dexterity on the mouth organ. They both took piano lessons, as was customary in those days, and I also started to learn much later on, when I was nine. My mother was an accomplished pianist and had an excellent soprano voice; she sang in many oratorios at various Portsmouth venues, but my father was fairly devoid of any artistic accomplishments. He did possess a sort of 'bathroom baritone' and was known to sing an awful ballad which began 'On the dewy green danced the elves of night' at office dinners. I have never heard of it since.

Paul and Olga attended Wimborne Road School, a primary – or elementary school as they were called then – within walking distance from home. Boys and Girls were separate, as was normal. Then, when Paul was eleven, he won a scholarship to the Boys' Southern Secondary School. My mother hated the idea of any of her children receiving state education, and when I reached the age of five I was sent to a small private school, 'Kentridge', known as 'Miss Brock's'. I could already read well and tell the time, and I remember being very bored when I saw 'The Cat sat on the Mat' type primer with which we were issued, for at home I was already avidly reading 'Tiger Tim's Weekly' and 'The Rainbow'. There were dancing classes at Kentridge after school, and I longed to join the other little girls whom I watched changing into their pink ballet shoes, and getting into their practice dresses with an important air. Sadly, dancing was an 'extra' and there were many more essential expenses to be addressed with a family of three growing children.

But even at that early age I loved to sing, and with a group of other small children enjoyed taking part in a spirited rendering of 'Nymphs and Shepherds' at a school concert. We had to have white dresses for this, and my mother made me one in white satin, with a row of sequins round the neck. Nobody else's dress had these, and I felt very superior.

There were many childhood illnesses about in those days, and vaccination against smallpox seemed to be the only preventative measure available. Both Olga and Paul caught scarlet fever and diphtheria and had to be cared for in an isolation hospital. Small as I was, I remember them, wrapped in blankets, being bundled into the waiting ambulance. These diseases, seldom heard of nowadays, could be life-threatening, and Olga was for a day or two placed on the 'danger list', but both of them eventually recovered fully. Poor Olga's beautiful long hair was cut off, and she never grew it again. I was kept well away from them as soon as they showed signs of illness, and luckily escaped infection. However, I made up for that by contracting measles and mumps (at the same time!) and suffered from bronchitis every winter. I remember being ill and confined to bed one Christmas Eve and my mother looking out of the window. 'He's coming!' she said, 'Here he is!' (meaning Santa Claus, of course), 'Let me see him!' I wheezed, trying to get out of bed. 'No, no, you mustn't,' she replied hurriedly, 'If you're don't go to sleep, he won't come!' That was enough for me, I obediently dropped off at once. When I awoke next morning, there was an enormous Christmas tree in the corner of the bedroom, decked with gleaming baubles and tinsel, and with a beautiful celluloid fairy doll at the top. She was dressed in frilled white crepe paper, liberally sprinkled with glitter, with a wand and lovely silver wings. How did my parents manage to get all this into the room without waking me? And decorate it, too. That is a piece of magic I have never forgotten.

We didn't hang out stockings to be filled – these were found to be much too small, so pillowcases fixed to the end of the bed were the order of the day. Not that we received loads of expensive presents – certainly not – bringing up three children was costly enough for our parents. But our biggest presents were Annuals – thick, copiously illustrated books full of stories and puzzles, issued by the publishers of our favourite comics. These usually cost about six shillings each, and were highly valued and appreciated by each one of us. Paul would receive the 'Schoolboy's Own' Annual, full of the exploits of Harry Wharton, Bob Cherry and Billy Bunter of the Remove at Greyfriars School, plus many exploits of daring-do. Olga would find in her pillowcase the girls' equivalent – 'Schoolgirl's Own Annual', containing similar tales, health and beauty hints, and stories of intrepid girls embarking on amazing adventures. My book would be the 'Pip and Squeak' annual, containing lots of stories, cartoons and competitions. It was based on the strip cartoon which appeared at that time in the *Daily Mirror* and featured the unlikely trio of 'Pip', 'Squeak' and 'Wilfred' – a dog, a penguin and a rabbit, who got into to all sorts of scrapes. I loved it. Two of the old annuals – rather dog-eared and well-thumbed – still have a place on my book shelves. There were many other small novelties in our pillowcases, but nothing else cost more than a few pence. It was the unwrapping and the surprise element that made it all so exciting. I once received a toy sweetshop fitted with a shelf of tiny jars of assorted sweets and minute tin scales for weighing them out. That was rather special.

In the autumn, my mother would say, looking at the calendar, "Goodness me, it's the middle of October already – time to think about making the Christmas puddings." She would clear the kitchen table, go to the larder, and begin getting out the ingredients. I would love to watch as she assembled all the delicious items which would go into this seasonal delicacy. There were fat, juicy raisins, sultanas and currants – all these had to be thoroughly washed and spread out on a clean tea towel to dry. Pre-packed and cleaned dried fruit did not exist in the nineteen-thirties, and the raisins had to be stoned – this was slow, laborious work, but they were much bigger and more luscious than the seedless variety which we know today. The most exciting thing, I thought, was the candied peel, which consisted of of crystalized orange and lemon halves, with big lumps of solid sugar still sticking to the inside. This had to be removed (I was allowed to eat a very tiny bit) and the peel chopped with a sharp knife into very small pieces. Olga always helped with all these preparations, but I was not old enough to use a knife, so watched the elaborate procedures with great interest, slyly abstracting a few raisins now and again when my mother's back was turned. Suet was bought from the butcher in a lump, which must be finely grated, sugar poured from its blue bag into a pan and weighed, flour sifted, eggs broken into another bowl and beaten, ready for use. Finally, all the ingredients were put together into a very large earthenware mixing bowl – now it was time for stirring. This was a very important stage in the procedure, as all the family must have their turn with the wooden spoon and make a wish as they stirred. I had to stand on a chair to do this, and it was very difficult, but I stirred as hard as I could, eyes firmly closed, and made my wish. I don't remember now what I wished for, but it was almost certainly something I hoped to get from Santa Claus when the time came. Wishes had to be kept secret, and nobody must be told what they were. When everyone had taken their turn, my mother finished the mixing, and added a little stout to make the consistency just right, but refused to put in a lucky sixpence or other charms as some people did, as she thought we might swallow them. She always made three puddings, considering all this work merited more than just the one on Christmas Day. The other two would appear on special occasions later in the New Year, one of them her birthday in January. The puddings were not tied up in a cloth and boiled, as was common practice, but the mixture was put into basins covered tightly with greaseproof paper and placed in saucepans of boiling water, where they simmered away for eight hours! What steam filled the kitchen – windows were opened however cold it was, and a boiling kettle kept ready to top up the water – the pans must not be allowed to boil dry. When they were cooked and cooled, they were sealed down with fresh paper and stored away at the back of the larder. It was all very exciting, and made Christmas seem just round the corner, though it was in fact weeks away.

I had an unconventional but rather splendid dolls' house which had originally been an open-fronted boot cupboard in my grandmother's house. It was made of solid mahogany and had a gable-shaped top which looked like a roof, and was divided into eight fairly large sections. These, painted and papered, made perfect rooms for the Ellis family, by which name my dolls were called. I played with it endlessly, changing the furniture round and re-dressing the dolls in the tiny garments devised by my mother and Olga. My favourite birthday present ever was a model bathroom for the dolls' house Behind the bath and wash basin were small reservoirs that could be filled with water, which came gushing out of the taps when you turned them on! I thought that quite amazing. When I went to play with friends who had superior dolls' houses with real fronts and windows (mine only had a curtain) I would examine *their* bathrooms and say, in a superior voice "Very nice . . . . . but *my* taps really *work* . . . ."

Treats in our family were fairly simple, and I remember the fortnightly delivery of a wooden crate of fizzy drinks manufactured by a firm called Cantrell and Cochrane, which was anticipated with enormous pleasure. There were six different flavours – ginger beer, of course, lemonade, orangeade, Cream Soda, limeade and – most delicious of all – a deep red concoction called Claret Cup. (though it sounds like one of today's 'alco-pops' it certainly contained no alcohol!). Enjoying one of these exotic beverages was really quite an occasion, and they were poured into special glasses, gloated over and drunk slowly with great relish. The delicious drinks had to last for a fortnight, till the next delivery was due, then the empty bottles and crate were put out for replacement. Those bottles were fascinating, closed with a sort of marble in the neck, held by a spring clip. Everything was recycled in those days – bottles were returned for cleansing and re-use. On all drinks bought at the shop, a penny was paid for each 'empty' returned, so children were keen to collect as many as they could to supplement their pocket money. You never saw a bottle lying about in the street to be smashed – pennies were scarce, and empty bottles a welcome source of revenue. There was even a rhyme which we chanted as we turned our skipping ropes:

'R. White's ginger beer goes off pop!
A penny on the bottle when you take it to the
s – h – o – p, SHOP!'

From a very early age I became used to a great deal of music in our house. There would be my mother playing the piano and learning various solo parts in oratorios which she would be performing in some local church or other, Paul and Olga practising, and precious (then, the very latest!) 78 records being played on a wind-up gramophone. This was a very superior and much cherished machine housed in a polished wooden cabinet on barley-twist legs. I remember standing on tiptoe and lifting the lid to look at the trade mark picture of the little dog sitting by the horn gramophone, listening to his master, hence the brand name of course, 'His Master's Voice'. Everyone enjoyed playing the gramophone, and among our more serious records we had a couple of humorous ones – our favourite, which made us roll on the floor with hysterical laughter was 'The Laughing Policeman', which has gone down in history, but the other, a raucous song called 'Why is the Bacon so Tough?' has – probably with good reason – faded into oblivion. Many of these records bore the 'Eclipse' label, and were bought from Woolworths for sixpence each. We would take turns to wind up the machine by means of a large handle at the side, and would laugh uproariously when it wound down, causing the record to grind slowly to a halt, turning a soprano voice to a bass one. Then, of course, there was the wireless – an imposing wooden affair with a curved top and fretwork front filled in with some sort of gauze material. This had to be carefully tuned, or terrible noises, oscillating and crackling, emanated from it. I'm not sure how it worked, but I know there was an 'accumulator' – a large, heavy glass box-like piece of acid-filled equipment which had to be taken to be recharged at intervals. We listened to lots of music on this, also the wonderful 'Children's Hour'. 'Toytown', with Larry the Lamb, Dennis the Dachshund and all those other lovable characters was my absolute favourite, and not to be missed. This wireless was eventually replaced by a mains-powered model when such things became available. Accumulators and oscillation were then things of the past.

Comics were delivered once a week and devoured avidly as soon as they came through the letter box. For Paul there was the *Rover* and the *Champion*, while Olga had the *Rainbow* and a small magazine called *Fairyland Tales*. For me I believe there was *Chicks' Own* and *Tiger Tim's Weekly*, in which I enjoyed the adventures of the animals in Mrs Bruin's school. In later years we progressed to *Film Fun, The Beano* and *The Dandy*, and I well remember the exploits of 'Keyhole Kate', 'Desperate Dan' and 'Ping – the Elastic Man'.

When I was five my tonsils became badly infected, and it was obvious that something must be done about it. Septic tonsils were automatically removed in those days, and mine were to be no exception.

The thought of her frail little child, frightened and alone, going into an austere hospital (as they were in the nineteen-thirties) for surgery, distressed my mother so much that our family doctor suggested that the operation might be carried out at home. I was at that time very thin and pale, suffering seasonally from bronchitis, and I believe my parents feared they might lose me if they let me out of their sight. So the event – unbelievable now – took place: my tonsils were removed on our kitchen table! In the light of modern day standards of surgery and technology, to say nothing of health and safety, this story sounds incredible, but I assure you that it's quite true. A very good surgeon, Mr Green, came to perform the procedure, and I made a full and speedy recovery. The deal kitchen table was scrubbed and covered with a white sheet, of course, and everything made as hygienic as possible, but even so, the whole thing seems bizarre. I clearly remember coming round from the anaesthetic (chloroform!), waking back in my bed, feeling very sick, with a terribly sore throat, and Paul appearing at my bedside with a jar in which a couple of gruesome pieces of flesh floatied in a murky liquid. 'D'you want to see your tonsils?' he enquired gleefully. 'No-oo-oo!' I wailed hoarsely, turning my face to the wall. But in spite of the extraordinary circumstances, the operation was obviously a success. At any rate, I was able to embark on a career as a singer years later!

Very few women carried their shopping home in those days. My mother would go to the grocer's shop with her list, give out the weekly order, plus any extras that took her eye, and the wooden box of groceries would be delivered later that day. Errand boys, who made the deliveries, were a common sight, pedalling along on their bicycles. These had small front wheels to accommodate large metal carriers emblazoned with the name of their shop, in which the provisions were carried. Absolutely everything could be delivered to your door if you so wished. As a little girl I loved going shopping with mother, and would perch on a high stool by the counter to watch the proceedings and look with longing at the row of glass-topped tins of biscuits at the front of the counter. I was sometimes rewarded by a quarter of a pound of 'iced gems' – tiny biscuits with stars of coloured icing on top – my favourites. It was the same routine at the butcher and the greengrocer – orders were given, and everything was delivered, usually on the same day. The baker's boy would call each morning with a large basket of fresh bread from which you selected the loaves you required. It was mostly white bread in those days – but *what* bread! Crusty cottage loaves, 'tins' and 'bloomers', milk bread, currant bread and rolls. We seldom had brown bread – indeed, it was looked upon as rather a treat to have a Hovis or Bermaline loaf, probably on a Sunday. As a small child I was particularly fond of farthing buns – yes, *four* for a penny! These were very small of course, brightly glazed, with plenty of currants, and all joined together, so that you usually bought several pennies worth and pulled them apart.

There were always parties for birthdays – at that time only for Paul and Olga, as I was rather too small; mine would come later. Paul's would mainly consist of a few of his best friends, who would gather round his Meccano set or model railway and become completely involved, emerging only for the typical birthday tea. Olga's parties would include all the old games – 'musical chairs', 'blind man's buff', and 'pinning the tail on the donkey', and all the little girls would be dressed in party frocks, with bows in their hair. How different were the refreshments provided in the days of the early thirties from those we know today. It was all so simple – sandwiches of egg and cress, cheese and tomato, some sausage rolls maybe, and of course – jellies – jellies were a must! And a birthday cake. No pizzas, burgers, or anything like that – no goody bags for guests to take home. Expectations were modest, and we found enormous pleasure in the smallest things. Just as well, perhaps, for we were maybe better equipped to cope with the deprivations that were to follow less than a decade hence.

My mother – like so many ordinary mothers in those days – didn't go out to work. Looking after three children, two at school and a younger one, cooking, dressmaking, shopping and cleaning the house took up much of her time. She had a 'girl' to do the 'rough' called Mabel, who occasionally took me out in the park in my pram, later my push-chair, or fetched me from school once I'd started at Miss Brock's. Young though I was, I have a distinct recollection of Mabel, who was a very willing but slightly simple girl. She would help my mother on wash day, lifting the clothes from the steaming copper and putting them through the mangle. No washing machines then!

When I look back and remember the kind of diet our family – and most others – enjoyed, I wonder why there was so little obesity – indeed, it was very rare. Steak and kidney puddings and pies, shepherd's pie, stews with dumplings, treacle puddings, suet puddings of all delicious kinds – these were the sort of meals we had daily, though in summer we did have plenty of salads. There was always a roast at weekends, Yorkshire puddings with beef, of course, and with lamb my mother always made a sort of flat suet pudding which was cooked in the fat from the joint till the top became brown and crispy – delicious – we hadn't heard of cholesterol then. Crisps and sweets were treats to be bought when pocket money allowed, and by no means available on a daily basis. And I suppose exercise played a big part in keeping us all reasonably slim. Walking or cycling to work or school, no television to flop in front of for whole evenings at a time, and the fact that children could disappear safely on their bikes with a packed lunch for a whole day at a time – this continual physical activity obviously contributed to our failure to put on excess weight. All the walking we did obviously took its toll upon our shoes, and whenever anyone had a new pair, 'protectors' would be applied to toes and heels before the shoes were worn The proprietary name for these was 'Segs' and they were usually bought in packets at Woolworths. My father would place the shoe to be attended to on a last – a heavy cast-iron appliance with two different sized feet for large or small shoes. A Seg was a metal, half-moon-shaped device about half an inch across, with short spikes on one side. This was hammered into the toe or heel of the sole, and would take all the hardest wear, saving – or 'protecting' – the original leather. I think different shaped ones could be bought for other areas of the sole. Quite an economy where three children were concerned, though they had their disadvantages, bringing complaints from my mother when they made scratches on her polished linoleum! In the summer we wore sandals or canvas shoes which had to be cleaned with a white block cleaner applied with a damp sponge, then put in the sun to dry. I remember being very fond of some white buckskin shoes which I was only allowed to wear on special occasions.

Dresses for parties were no problem for us. Our Auntie Ellie, my mother's sister, who lived near Birmingham, had three daughters – Ena, Phyllis and Eileen. She was married to Uncle Alfred Cotton (always known as Alphonso – I don't know why) who was a highly successful businessman, and they were a very wealthy family. The little girls wore their party dresses a few times, then they were sent to us. It was so exciting when the parcels arrived, and we tried them on. Olga once had a beautiful low-waisted orange crepe-de-chine dress with a belt fastened by a diamante buckle, and a frilled skirt. There was also a lovely embroidered pale blue taffeta dress which fitted her exactly, and a pale pink one for me in finest voile. We wore our 'new' party dresses with great pride. They probably came from Harrods or Cavendish House, in Cheltenham. Our parents could never have afforded anything like that. In fact, all our everyday and school dresses were made at home. My mother would work far into the night at her hand-operated Singer sewing machine, stitching away at gingham, polka dot or 'Tobralco' cotton print so that we could have new dresses for some occasion or other. Olga always asked for checks, but I preferred floral designs. I had a particular favourite with white daisies on a pink background, which I wore and wore until I grew out of it. A blue dress with white daisies was made to replace it, but it never had the same place in my affection. On laundry day the dresses would be washed – by hand, of course – then starched with 'Robin' patent starch, put through a big old mangle with wooden rollers and pegged out on the clothes line. When the dresses were dry, they'd be brought in, 'damped down' and rolled up, ready for ironing. That was done with flat irons – electric ones were a very rare luxury in those days. My mother had two flat irons – one would be heating on the gas ring – the other in use, and the kitchen table would be covered with a thick ironing blanket, scorched in places from constant use. I remember sitting on a high stool and watching her. As she re-arranged the dress between strokes, she would rest the iron on an old up-turned 'Mansion Polish' tin, and when it became too cool she would exchange it for the one on the gas ring. We don't realise how lucky we are now! My dresses always had knickers to match, as I was wont to do handstands on the spur of the moment, and was often to be found upside down trying out some acrobatic feat. Matching knickers were considered to be more respectable.

I liked going with my mother on the tram to the big shopping centre, maybe to buy material for summer dresses, or a new pair of shoes for small feet that were growing fast. We'd often go for afternoon tea to a rather smart café called 'The Mikado', which name became significant for me many years later when I joined the D'Oyly Carte Opera Company and sang 'Yum-Yum' in the Gilbert and Sullivan opera of that name. There was a raised pool in the centre of the café filled with exotic fish and a fountain. I was allowed to leave my place at the table and watch them (having first asked permission). That's one thing we always had to do – we were never allowed to leave the table without asking 'Can I get down?' first – quite a civilised request, I think. (Of course, it *should* have been '*May* I?' but the intention was right.)

We never went without our summer holiday – travelling all the way to Hayling Island, which is right next door to Portsmouth! But that didn't matter – the exciting trip by ferry made it seem like going to another world. And what an idyllic spot it was then – deserted beaches and winding country lanes fringed with brambles weighed down with luscious, ripe blackberries, for it was always the end of August and the first week of September when we took our fortnight's holiday. It seemed to me that every day was warm and sunny, though I'm sure that wasn't really the case. A trunk containing all the things we needed was sent on in advance by rail for two-and-sixpence, and was always there waiting for us when we arrived. A family of five got through an awful lot of clothes in a fortnight, and the water availability at our holiday venue meant that only essential laundry was done. We found it very exciting getting settled in to our 'coach bungalow', which consisted of two railway carriages set at right angles in a plot of rather wild garden. The interior was bright with glossy cream paint, and the crockery a brilliant orange edged with black. Windows were opened and closed with leather straps, just as they had been when the carriages were in service on the railway, and the old seats converted into comfortable bunks. Cooking was done on a strange, ancient oil stove, which emitted a loud 'glump' when you were least expecting it. My mother once made blackberry jam from brambles we'd picked in the lane – where she found the jars and how on earth we got it home has long since faded from my memory. Jars of jam are not the easiest things to transport safely on public transport.

The 'bungalow' was in the grounds of a house owned by a slightly eccentric lady called Mrs McCarry, and water had to be fetched from a well, which necessitated passing her door. Fetching water often resulted in our being invited in to see her latest needlework extravaganzas. Her sitting room was crowded with all manner of handmade novelties – dressed dolls, fancy pincushions, lace-trimmed lavender bags, satin handkerchief sachets, cushion covers and nightdress cases. Goodness knows what she did with them all, though I expect she probably sold quite a few to her holiday guests. We usually bought one or two items, and I particularly remember a large South American doll with turban and big gold ear-rings, and a brightly-coloured skirt which discreetly provided a receptacle for soiled linen. We had her for ages. After we had enjoyed our railway coaches for two or three years, Mrs McCarry had the site cleared, and a conventional brick bungalow built, with all mod cons. We continued to take our holidays there, and it was very comfortable and convenient of course, but to us it lacked the magic of the old coaches.

All the family were excellent swimmers except me – and I was learning fast. With an inflated rubber ring round my waist I would go fearlessly out of my depth, or half a mile or so out to sea on my father's shoulders. It was all the rage in those days to wear knitted swim suits – or bathing costumes as we called them then. My mother would buy special wool, guaranteed not to sag or shrink – Paton and Baldwin's 'Holiday' wool, I think it was called – and spend hours knitting jazzy numbers for Hayling Island. My favourite was brown and orange striped – I must have looked like a large bumble bee, but I fancied myself no end. Coloured rubber bathing caps adorned with garish flowers were the order of the day, and because the beach was partly pebbly, we often wore rubber bathing shoes as well. We had no expensive beach toys – buckets and spades, certainly, and these were very different from those of today. There was no plastic as we know it now, and spades were either made entirely from wood, or with wooden handles and a metal blade. Buckets were tin, brightly painted, and decorated with Walt Disney characters or other similar designs. Our favourite possession was an inflated and much patched car inner tube in which we floated and splashed in turn. There weren't any fancy sunscreens or Ambre Solaire – if any of us suffered from sunburn, a lavish application of calomine lotion was the remedy.

We often had the beach to ourselves and regarded any other people who approached our territory with proprietary disdain, but we were amused by a strange, old-fashioned-looking family who came down regularly for a swim. There were the sombrely-attired parents and about five demure daughters with waist-length hair. We would watch discreetly, giggling amongst ourselves as the girls removed layer after layer of cotton petticoats, long drawers and stockings, and donned modest swimming costumes. We called them 'The Tribe of Israel' – I'm not sure why. The girls usually had a brief swim, then struggled back into their all-enveloping undergarments and high-necked, long-sleeved dresses, then the family left. It was obviously an operation designed solely for health-giving reasons; there was certainly no evidence of any enjoyment – no laughter or splashing. We were intrigued. I was glad not to wear all that underwear – a cotton frock and knickers were the most I had on all summer, plus a pair of sandals.

In addition to the fortnight at Hayling Island, we spent all our summer Sundays on the beach at Southsea, weather permitting, of course. Everyone cycled – except me, at that stage – I rode on a carrier behind my mother. All the picnic things were strapped on to the bikes, plus swimming costumes and towels, and even a small rickety tent. How we carried it all, I really can't imagine. The Sunday roast would be cooked on the Saturday, and that would be taken too, to be eaten cold with salad. I remember quite clearly eating cold roast lamb, salad and new potatoes off enamel plates on the beach – or in the tent if it was windy. The part of the beach where we pitched our tent was was stony; it was sandy nearer the water. This was a good thing in many ways, where eating was concerned, for there's nothing more annoying than sand blowing into your food. We were usually joined by the O'Brien family – Mr and Mrs and their twin sons, Michael and Peter, who wore startling black and yellow striped bathing costumes, and looked like a couple of skinny wasps. We splashed in the sea and played together all day, reluctant to leave when the sun began to set.

On one occasion a very exciting event happened – we heard a deafening noise and my father shouting, "Look, look!" as the bright red Supermarine, winner of the Schneider Trophy, sped along the sea in front of our eyes. Little did we know then that the famous Spitfire, which was to play such part in our lives in the not so distant future would be developed from this remarkable plane. There was always something interesting to be seen from Southsea beach, for many of the ocean-going liners and naval warships sailed that way from Southampton or Portsmouth respectively. My mother, who was born and brought up in Cowes, had watched the RMS 'Titanic' sail past on her ill-fated maiden voyage a couple of decades previously. If we spotted a really big vessel approaching, not far out to sea, we'd shout, "Move up the beach!" and gather all our things together, for the wash from the ship could be considerable and all our possessions might soon be floating away if we didn't carry them up to a safer place.

Men would come along the beach at intervals, selling various items – sun hats, eye-shades, buckets and spades, sweets – and wonderful 'surprise packets' which I always begged my parents to buy for me. They usually said, 'No – they're only full of rubbish!' but occasionally they gave in, and I would open the large paper bag rapturously, taking out one tawdry item after another – celluloid dolls, soft coloured balls made of strange crocheted cotton and stuffed with sawdust, which very soon leaked out, games, some garishly-coloured sweets and perhaps a rather dubious lollipop. I gloated over this collection of shoddy rubbish with enormous delight – it seemed like treasure trove to a five or six-year-old.

We were always sorry to pack up all our things at the end of another wonderful Sunday, load up the bicycles and set off on the journey home. Another week of school stretched gloomily ahead. But we reminded ourselves we'd be back there again in a week's time – though a week is an awfully long time when you're young. Those carefree summer days on the beach were very happy times.. ... I remember them as if they were yesterday.

A CHANGE OF SCENE

Every promotion that came my father's way involved a move to another area, and when I was seven he was relocated to Croydon. So it was farewell to Portsmouth, then the excitement of a new home and a change of school for all of us. Not to live by the sea was a strange idea – what would we do on summer weekends? Wouldn't we be able to swim any more? What a disturbing thought. It was customary to rent a house in those times – home ownership was still comparatively rare. In any case, owing to my father's work it would have been impossible to settle in any one area, so a three-year lease was usually secured on a suitable property, and this time we found ourselves at number eleven, Nursery Close, Shirley. It was quite a change for us: from a rather old-fashioned Edwardian villa we moved into a modern semi-detached house with an Ideal boiler to heat the water, a large garden which backed on to Thomas Butcher's lovely nursery, and a monkey puzzle tree at the front.

What excitement there was, exploring the house and garden, and the new neighbourhood. Were there any children of my age in the road, I wondered? I soon made friends with a little girl across the way – Elizabeth Alderton – known as 'Dilly', and we still exchange Christmas cards to this very day, although she has lived in Canada for decades, and we haven't met for over sixty years! What games of cowboys and indians we played, and what blissful hours were spent with our model farms and dolls' houses. We loved to draw, too. Dilly would come over for the whole day sometimes, during the school holidays, and we would sit on my bedroom floor drawing, painting and cutting out from books of paper dolls, oblivious of time. My mother would bring us some lunch, and always for pudding – bananas and custard! We would have nothing else.

When Dilly and I were old enough, we were allowed to go to the children's cinema on Saturday morning at the Odeon, West Wickham. We'd catch a bus – it was a couple of miles or so – feeling very grown-up, and get off just outside the cinema, where we'd pay our sixpences to sit upstairs, casting superior glances at the queue for the fourpennies down in the stalls. We would try to sit in the front row, where we could drop our sweet wrappers down on the lesser mortals from time to time. There was always a long cowboy or adventure film, a cartoon, and a serial. How we cheered Tom Mix or Buck Jones or Ken Maynard, screamed with laughter at the cartoon, and sat on the edge of our seats with bated breath during the exciting episode of the serial, which invariably ended with the hero in some impossibly dangerous situation. Just as we could bear no more suspense, on the screen appeared 'Continued Next Week'. We breathed sighs of relief. 'Flash Gordon' was on regularly, and one of our favourites; we'd discuss the episode all the way home. Would he escape from the clutches of evil Ming the Merciless? How could we possibly wait a whole week to see what happened next?

New local schools had to be found, of course. Paul was accepted by Whitgift, in Croydon, and it was Olga's turn to be sent to a private school – Hadley House, in Addiscombe, where she met her lifelong friend Vera King. As for me – my mother was upset at the idea of an elementary school until she saw the Benson School in Shirley. It was modern, well appointed, and stood in the middle of a very pleasant residential area. Some of the children were even being dropped off at the school gates by car! Not many people had cars then, so, much reassured, she agreed to my attending, and it proved to be a very good decision. School hours were from nine till twelve, and two till four – fifteen, so I would go home for lunch. I suppose it was the best part of a mile from our house, so I must have walked about four miles a day – that's twenty miles a week!

Wonderful exercise, certainly.

Shirley was little more than a village in the early thirties; there were woods and country lanes, and even a windmill – though not a working one – just up the road. The Shirley hills were a regular place for walks, and the whole area had a rural feel. We missed the sea, naturally, but there was plenty of lovely countryside nearby in those days, and our parents promised us a seaside holiday when the time came. There were some useful little shops in Shirley – I remember a drapers' shop called Blennerhassetts, which seemed to stock absolutely everything, a post office and a confectioner's called Dumonts – a large jolly lady whom we called 'Auntie Dumont' was the proprietor. There was a butcher, where my mother placed her weekly order, a greengrocer, an ironmonger, and a small dress shop called 'Janet's', and above all, a library – a facility I could not possibly manage without, as I read every minute of my spare time. The only disadvantage was that you could not take books back on the same day as you borrowed them, and I had always finished mine in an hour or so. It seemed an eternity to wait until you were able to change them. I was taken to the local hairdresser to have my hair cut about once a month; I always wanted to grow it, but was never allowed to. Olga had had lovely long hair which she wore in plaits when she was younger, but in spite of my pleas, I was stuck with short hair and a fringe. There was no point in arguing about it. I often got my own way, but not in this case.

Croydon was then a pleasant small town, by no means a suburb of London as it is now, and just a penny bus ride away (twopence for adults). We would catch the 194 to East Croydon every Saturday afternoon and walk down George Street. I remember noticing a large sign on the bridge advertising a local garage. It read: 'G.L. Sparrow & Sons – Wing and Body Repairs' – we laughed every time we saw it. We'd stroll round the shops, buy produce at the Crown Hill market (most things were reduced late on Saturdays), and finally – a big treat – we'd have tea and wonderful cakes at Kennard's, a big department store. A big tray of tea would arrive, with large silver-plated pot and hot water jug, scones and jam, and a two-tiered cake stand with a mouth-watering assortment of cakes and pastries – Bath buns, sprinkled with crystals of sugar, Chelsea buns, enticingly rolled and stuffed with sultanas, cream horns, chocolate éclairs and jam puffs. I gazed, round-eyed, spoilt for choice.

Kennard's was a wonderful store, we thought. Every so often they would have a 'Blue Pencil Day' when all prices were slashed, and we went to hunt for bargains. There was a bargain basement, too, where all sorts of things were permanently cheap, and a children's hat department (yes, children wore hats in those days) with a big sign saying 'Kids' Lids' which at the age of nine or so I thought excruciatingly funny. Shetland pony rides took place down a little lane at the side of the store, and I sometimes treated myself if I had any pocket money left after spending most of it in the bargain basement on drawing books and crayons. If I hadn't, someone usually took pity on me and made up the deficit – after all, it was only threepence.

In Allders, another large store opposite, there was a display of Shirley Temple dolls of all sizes, arranged in a special glass display case. Every single Saturday I insisted on going to look at them, and would stand there for ages taking in every detail of their beautiful curls and dresses. These were all exact copies of copies of what the juvenile star actually wore. The dolls were fairly expensive – from fourteen shillings and sixpence for the small size, up to an enormous thirty-two and six for the largest. How I longed for one of my own, but surely such an expensive item could never be afforded. But, lo and behold – next birthday, there she was – gift-wrapped, on the breakfast table. Not the most expensive one, that would have been too much to expect, but I thought her perfect. She had real hair, dressed in ringlets, which you could actually comb, and was provided with a set of curlers for refreshing her curls when necessary. I was in seventh heaven, and took her everywhere. I still have my doll today, slightly the worse for wear, together with all the small dresses made for her by Olga, and painstakingly copied from my Shirley Temple picture books.

I liked the Benson School very much, and at eight won prizes of books for English and Art. I have them still – 'Black Beauty' and 'Little Women'. Every day, in arithmetic lessons, we would all chant our tables together until they became second nature to us. Even today, if anyone asks me, for instance, what eleven times twelve is, I will unhesitatingly say 'A hundred and thirty-two' – it's there for ever in my memory. There's something to be said for learning 'by rote', however boring it may seem at the time. There were spelling tests every day, and words spelled incorrectly had to be written out ten times; when you'd done that they were usually impressed firmly in your memory.

The Croydon epidemic of typhoid fever in 1937 caused everyone great anxiety, for the illness was serious, and could even prove fatal. More and more cases were announced daily, and the mother of one of the boys in my class succumbed to the illness. He came to school, but was sent home immediately; no risk of infection could be taken where children were concerned. Altogether three hundred and forty-one cases were reported before the source of the disease was established. It was the contaminated water supply from one of the reservoirs which was causing the problem, and this, when remedied, halted the epidemic, and we all breathed sighs of relief.

I marvel now at what was required of children at such an early age – essays -or 'compositions' as they were called – were set regularly, and a surprising amount of grammar taught. We would labour over our exercise books, dipping pens into inkwells and painstakingly filling two or three pages with careful script, taking care not to make a smudge or drop a blot. We knew that any such defacement of the page would be ringed round with red pencil, and marks lost. Our teacher would often give us a title and ask us to write a story about it, or perhaps we'd be given a final sentence, in which case we would have to write a composition ending with those words. I still have my old dog-eared exercise book containing some of my ten-year-old efforts. Here's one of them – we must have been given the title 'Rescue!' The date is the seventh of February, 1938. I was ten.

Rescue!

Day was breaking as I regained consciousness, but for some time I could not remember where I was.

I saw the mouth of the cave into which I had been swept, and then I remembered the terrible disaster of yesterday.

For hours I had clung to the wreckage of the ship on which I had been a passenger, and I wondered how many of the passengers and crew had been saved.

The previous day had been one of terror for many people, for the ship, travelling in the fog, had gone off her course and struck a reef.

I rose from the stone floor of the cave, my back ached, for I had been lying there for many hours. I staggered, somewhat dazed, out into the brilliant sunlight, and saw that the fog had cleared, and the sea was calm.

I wandered along the deserted sandy beach, and saw some wreckage of my old ship. Suddenly I saw a black shape on the horizon and I shaded my eyes to see it better, and as it came nearer I realized it was a ship of some kind. "What can I do to attract its attention?" I wondered, and as if in answer, a piece of dried seaweed blew along the beach in front of me. "I'll build a beacon, and set light to it," I said aloud, and set to work at once. It did not take long, and I lit it by rubbing two sharp stones together.

It flared up and soon I saw the ship turning in my direction. The minutes I waited semed like hours, but in spite of that, the ship stopped, and a rowing boat came up.

The men rowing took me in, and back to the ship, and before long I found myself sailing for home.

That epic story filled nearly four pages of my exercise book, in large sloping writing. I got good marks for it, but the teacher wrote in the margin *'Was no search made for the other passengers?'* which I considered unnecessary. He ought to have been impressed by the fact that I made no spelling mistakes. I can't help wondering how many ten-year-olds of today could spell 'unconsciousness'? And cope with the punctuation? That was entirely due to the excellent education we received at the Benson School. Although our imagination was allowed full reign, we were expected to set down our ideas coherently, with due attention to spelling and grammar. The tale is reproduced exactly as it was written; nothing has been corrected or edited. Moreover, modern children would have biros, and would not have to endure the trauma of those wooden penholders fitted with long pointed nibs which scattered ink spots indiscriminately over our work if we were not careful. Blotting paper was a necessity – turning a page and forgetting to use it could be a disaster.

Another masterpiece is dated the twenty-eighth of March, the same year. Here, we were obviously given the finishing sentence to our composition: 'Such was its unfortunate ending.' This is my attempt:

The Milk Jug's Story

The table was set for tea. A fire flickered in the grate, Suddenly, the large brown teapot in the corner of the table, cleared his throat, and prepared to address the other china thus: "It is very dull on this table, waiting for tea to begin, so I suggest that someone should tell a story."

The crockery applauded the idea, so the milk jug was chosen

"Mine is not an adventure story, but a story of one of my old friends. My pattern is not the same as yours, for I do not belong to your teaset.

When we were ready to be packed up with paper and shavings, a vase knocked against me. He apologised, and we got into conversation.

Just then, the lid of the packing case was closed, and with a jolt, we were lifted into what we thought was a van, and soon we arrived at our destination.

We were unpacked, and set on shelves. A few days later, some gypsies came in, intending to buy prizes for their fair, and you may be sure that our hearts were beating very quickly as they looked about the shelves. Were we to be parted?

At last the gypsies took us and a few more articles, paid for us, and started back to their camp. Here we were arranged on a 'Hoop-La' stall. Lots of people came flocking round and trying to throw rings over us. One man, who seemed to be a good shot, aimed at me, and I found myself with a wooden ring round me.

I was taken and given to the man, and I watched tensely as the man had another try, and to my delight, my friend was won.

The man turned, and departed, but a person knocked his arm. The vase fell, and smashed.

"And," said the jug, "Such was its unfortunate ending."

Enthralling stuff!

There were more than forty children to a class, boys and girls, for Benson was a mixed school, unlike the separate sex school that Paul and Olga had attended in Portsmouth. But in spite of this, there seemed to be excellent discipline. Of course, there was always The Cane. In our small school world, the prospect of receiving that unspeakable punishment provided as effective a deterrent as the threat of a nuclear weapon in the wider world of today. It was hardly ever used – in my four years at the Benson I only heard of two senior boys summoned to the Head Teacher's office to receive the unmentionable punishment, and that event was spoken of in hushed voices, such was the ignominy and disgrace connected with it. "Have you heard?" one child 'in the know' whispered to another, "So-and-so got *The Cane* this morning!" There was a sharp intake of breath and an expression of horror. "*No!*" came the incredulous reply, "Did he *really?*" And the word would go round. I don't mean to say that we felt under threat – far from it – for we all realised that this shameful sentence was only carried out when the most heinous crime was committed, and the vast majority of us, though a bit naughty at times, were on the whole fairly well-behaved.

During our fifteen minute break from lessons, both morning and afternoon, we played all sorts of games in the playground, many of which were seasonal. There were marbles at a certain time of year, played by both boys and girls, and we all had wonderful collections in a great variety of colours. Most treasured were the 'blood alleys' – white marbles streaked with scarlet, which were the rarest and most sought after. One day tragedy struck. The bell rang, signifying the end of break and time to form into a line to return to the classroom, and I was just hurrying to obey when my bag of marbles broke and my precious treasures were scattered far and wide. What a disaster! I tried to gather up a few, but had to obey the bell, so most were left strewn over the playground. Of course, they had vanished by the time we came out of school, though I did find one or two – but not my precious blood alley! Then the craze for marbles would wane and some other pastime would come into fashion. Although one thinks of them more as Victorian playthings than toys of the thirties, spinning tops would emerge and take their place in the playground – yo-yos, too – and how superior it was to possess a *whistling* yo-yo! These spun up and down their strings giving out a loud whistling sound, drawing everyone round to watch with admiration and envy. There were always skipping games played by the girls, and of course 'The Farmer's in his Den'. This was played in a ring, with one girl in the centre as the Farmer. The others would join hands and walk round, singing:

> '*The Farmer's in his Den, the Farmer's in his den,*
> *Hi-tiddly-i-ti, the Farmer's in his den.*

Then: *The Farmer wants a wife, the Farmer wants a wife,*
> *Hi-tiddly-i-ti, the Farmer wants a wife.'*

At that point the 'Farmer' would choose one of the girls from the ring and pull her into the centre of the circle. The chant would begin again, this time 'The Wife wants a Child' and the 'Child' would be chosen. Then it would be 'the Child wants a Nurse', the Nurse wants a Dog' and finally 'the Dog wants a Bone' which would be the final part of the game. It doesn't sound wildly exciting, but it had a catchy tune and there was a lot of laughing and ridicule when the 'Bone' was chosen. Skipping was a fine art. There were many rhymes we sang in sing-song voices as we took turns either turning the rope or participating in the action. A popular one, sung to the tune of the 'Keel Row' was:

'The cat's got the measles, the mumps and the chicken pox,
Scarlatina,
Concertina,
Water on the brain!'

Two girls would swing the rope backwards and forwards as another jumped, then when 'Water on the brain' came up, the rope would be turned completely, very fast, three times, and the girl jumping had to look out! If she got caught by the rope she was 'out' and it was someone else's turn. We played a lot of these singing games, but the boys were usually engaged in something rather rougher. Scabby knees were the order of the day, and tumbles on the asphalt playground were a regular occurrence. A good scab on the knee was a thing to be cherished, and there was a certain stage in its development when you could prise it off – that was an interesting event. Woe betide you if you tried to do so before it was ready! "Leave it alone!" my mother would say if she saw me trying to lever a scab off surreptitiously. The temptation was irresistible.

The Benson School had been built, fairly recently I assume, on a field, and beyond the asphalted playground there were still areas of rough grass and bushes. This gave great scope for games, and the boys would set up camp in a selected area, chase the girls round the playground, (I took care not to run too fast!) capture them, and drag them into their lair. Nothing untoward happened there

– we just tried to escape, and ran for our lives, only to be caught again. There was a lot of rough and tumble, and we were all fairly breathless when the bell rang.

I used to walk to school along the Wickham Road and up Spring Park Road, where there was a tempting sweet shop cum general store half way up on the right hand side, called, not surprisingly 'Spring Park Stores'. I didn't always have much pocket money available, but even if you only had a farthing (a quarter of a penny) there was something you could spend it on. Small, square blocks of some gooey fruit-flavoured stuff called 'Fruity Chews' were available at a farthing each. All the sweets we bought with our limited pocket money were very inexpensive. Sherbert Fountains (or 'Dabs and Suckers' as they were sometimes called) consisted of yellow bags of sherbert with a hollow stick of liquorice sticking out of one corner and a lollipop out of the other. So you could either dab the lollipop in the sherbert or suck it up through the liquorice – hence the name! These were very cheap – I believe a penny each, and manufactured by Barretts, the confectioner, as almost all inexpensive, children-orientated sweets were. You could always buy a pennyworth – or even a half-pennyworth of boiled sweets – acid drops, pear drops, and some strange pink and yellow ones called 'rhubarb and custard' drops. Then there were liquorice rolls – long ribbons of liquorice rolled up tightly into a reel, with a sweet in the middle. Bubble gum, usually banned at school, was a favourite as we rudely blew bubbles at one another, and gobstoppers – enormous sweets which completely filled your mouth and prevented all speech for about ten minutes, were good value, as they lasted for ages. As you sucked them they changed colour, and we used to take them out of our mouths at intervals to see what stage they had reached – perhaps not a terribly good thing to do with grubby hands. I remember a peculiar craze when everyone was sucking liquorice root – we all seemed to become addicted to it, and it finally had rather unfortunate results, for there were many stomach upsets, and it became forbidden to bring it into school. It wasn't even particularly nice, so it was odd that it became so popular. We were soon back to our old favourites.

There was always assembly to start the day, with brief prayers and hymns, then we would march off to our classrooms. Every Monday morning we were all asked to bring two pence-halfpenny, which we gave to the class teacher. This entitled us to a two-thirds of a pint bottle of milk every break time. In the winter the milk sometimes arrived partly frozen, and the milk monitor of the week would take the bottles from the crate and line them up along the top of the big old-fashioned radiator. By the time the bell sounded for break, the milk was drinkable and we were able to push our straws though the perforated circle in the cardboard top. There were monitors for everything – to give out books, collect them up, clean the blackboard, open the windows with a long pole, and – requiring the greatest skill of all – to fill up the china inkwells which were set into each desk top. This needed a steady hand and a good eye. The ink, which when you got to the bottom of the inkwell, tended to clog up your pen nib and make blots, was made from a powder, to which water was added and well mixed. I suppose that accounted for the sediment that collected if the ink was not regularly replenished.

Nearly every day, weather permitting, we had 'drill' in the playground. After ten minutes or so of strenuous physical exercises four teams were selected, and with a class of nearly fifty, there were about a dozen pupils in each. Team captains were chosen, and gave out red, blue, green and yellow bands. Then followed various games in which the teams would compete against one another in relay races, jumping or ball games. Each win scored points and there was great completion between teams to see who would gain the highest score at the end of the session. There was a lot of shouting and cheering as players were encouraged to greater efforts. When time was up, the coloured team bands were collected and we formed lines to return to the classroom. I think the teachers relied upon this period of intense activity to encourage us to let off steam, after which we would be more inclined to simmer down and apply ourselves to arithmetic or spelling in a more docile frame of mind.

I loved singing, and we certainly had plenty of that. We worked our way through the National Song Book, spreading our patriotism impartially throughout the United Kingdom, from 'Hearts of Oak' and 'Ye Banks and Braes' to 'Danny Boy' and 'All Through the Night'. One very hot summer afternoon remains clearly in my memory. Even now, if I close my eyes and concentrate, I can be transported back to a day when the whole school was assembled in the hall to sing. We juniors had given spirited renderings of 'Dashing Away With a Smoothing Iron' and 'Drink to Me Only With Thine Eyes', then it was the seniors' turn. How big and grown-up they seemed to me then, yet none were older than eleven. They started to sing, and I was simply entranced. Their song was 'Linden Lea' by Vaughan Williams, and I thought it the most sublime music I'd ever heard. It still evokes that hot, sleepy summer afternoon whenever I hear it, and it would certainly be one of my eight 'Desert Island Discs'.

At the end of term there would be a concert for parents – some singing and recitations perhaps, and a short play. On one occasion my class were all to be bees, which posed quite a challenge for our mothers, who had to make the costumes. Mine was equal to the occasion, and I was soon fitted out with a smart velvet brown and orange striped suit, wire-framed wings in silvery gauve, and a brown skull-cap bearing two perky antennae. When I put this on at the dress rehearsal I felt very superior, as many of the other mothers hadn't seemed to bother very much, and some very odd attempts at bee outfits appeared, some even made of brown paper! At another concert we performed some sort of sixteenth century play, in which I was cast as the aristocratic 'Lady Ombersley'. For this my mother cut down an old blue velvet evening gown (probably from Auntie Ellie) and made it into a very credible Tudor costume, with ruched sleeves and a pearl-trimmed neckline. She even managed to construct a gable-style head-dress with long lace veil. Looking back on everything she did for me, I'm not sure if I ever thanked her enough. She certainly had little over from the housekeeping to spend on such things, probably less than some of the mothers who hadn't bothered with their children's costumes. Everything was contrived from what was available, but whenever there was any school event, she always made sure that I had the best she could provide.

There was a Brownie pack at the Benson School, in which I was enrolled with solemn ceremony. I felt quite proud, dressed in my new light brown cotton uniform with leather belt, darker brown tie, and rather strange brown woollen hat. With my left hand on the magic Toadstool, my right hand giving the official Brownie salute, and watched by Brown Owl, Tawny Owl and the rest of the pack, I gravely recited my vows: "I promise to do my best, to do my duty to God and the King, to help other people every day, especially those at home." Brown Owl acknowledged this statement by pinning on to my tie a shining gold (brass) badge in the shape of a sprite, and I was a Brownie. Every Tuesday we would take our sandwiches and stay on after school to indulge in all sorts of activities and games. There were four 'Sixes' in our Brownie pack, and each had a leader, known as a 'Sixer'. Being a slightly bossy individual I soon found myself chosen to be a Sixer – of the 'Pixies' – the others were 'Fairies', 'Elves' and 'Gnomes', I believe – how incredibly unsophisticated all this sounds today. But that's just how we were then, and we loved every minute of it.

There was such freedom for us children. In the summer, except on Brownie evenings, I would hurry home after school, have my tea, then rush off to the park to play with my friends. There was only one proviso: I had to be home by seven-thirty sharp, not a minute later. Spring Park, in Shirley, was a wonderful place to play, with a huge area of grass for games, and a copse of silver birch trees where wild *orchids* grew! *Orchids* – in a *suburban park!* It seems unbelievable nowadays, when we are lucky to find any even in remote rural locations.

I remember many of the children in my class; there was the form captain, Audrey Brooker, a rather serious, sporty girl; the twins – Jean and Pam Viall, bright and quick at lessons, and one poor girl – believe it or not – who rejoiced in the name of 'Mavis Muddle' – how did she cope with that in later life, I wonder? Probably got married very young, I should think. One of the boys had an equally unfortunate name – John Crapp – rather difficult to imagine starting out on a successful career with a handicap like that. Stella Sander was the class 'dunce', though I have since come to realise that she was more lazy than stupid. Then there was Ian Chuter – a genius at arithmetic – his hand would be up to give the answer before the rest of us had worked out what the question meant. Pammy Harrison, a small, rather wizened girl, driven to school each day in an expensive car, seemed to have some sort of bladder problem, which resulted in her being given rather a wide berth where seating was concerned. A succession of strange inventions made from Meccano were brought in at regular intervals by an earnest boy called David Lovatt and demonstrated at length to the class. I wonder if he became a technological wonder later on. Douglas McCabe was a canny Scots lad, I remember, and then of course, there was Eric Smyth – more of him anon.

Once a week there was 'Country Dancing' for all of us – boys included – outside if fine, otherwise in the school hall. To the scratchy sound of a wind-up gramophone we would frolic with varying degrees of proficiency through 'Haste to the Wedding' and 'Circassian Circle' and 'Shepherds Hey'. Although, in the thirties, children remained children for much longer than is the case today, there was already an awareness of the charms of the opposite sex! I was very much taken with the afore-mentioned Eric Smyth, a tall, fair-haired, blue-eyed lad, and was always working out a way to get him for my dancing partner. I very often managed this, to the chagrin of his many other admirers. One Valentine's Day I plucked up my courage and sent him a garish card covered with hearts – though when accused, I vehemently denied having anything to do with it! I don't think he was fooled for a moment, though. Sorting through a lot of old exercise books, photographs and papers, I actually came across a bundle of ancient diaries, which included a very dog-eared one for 1939. Some of it is written in pencil, and is now almost illegible, but there are a few entries in ink which graphically describe my juvenile infatuation with the handsome Eric, discreetly referred to as 'E.S.'.

Thursday, February 2nd:
Painting in morning. Sewing in afternoon. 3.45. Country Dancing, <u>*Had E.S. for partner. Jolly good time.*</u>
Thursday, February 9th:
Hooray! Painting in the morning. nice needlework in the afternoon. Best lesson of all – Country Dancing. Had E.S. Better than ever.

There is a special reference to the February 14th event:

Tuesday, February 14th
Red letter Day! Sent a Valentine to E.S. !!! Small congregation of boys waited for me outside the gates! E.S. looked so charming!

(*Charming?* What a strange word for a ten-year-old to use! Then it states 'continued in Memo' as there is obviously not room for the following ecstatic entry in the proper place:)

Memo: Tues (ctd) Best day Thursday. He found out and keeps it in his pocket. Seems to like me much better, I'm so pleased.

Friday, February 17th:
Boo! Went in hall. E.S. was out of sight 2 rows back and he could not see me. Very dull. No singing. Rotten nature study about clouds.

Here the passionate love affair seems to have petered out, as apart from an entry on Shrove Tuesday which reads '*Had some pancakes. Jolly nice*' the diary comes to an end. The momentous events which were to follow later that year are not recorded.

Our three-year lease on the house in Nursery Close came to an end, and was not available for renewal, and my father was still based in Croydon, so we moved to number twelve, Wickham Road, not very far away. This time the house was in a terrace, probably built in the twenties on land which had previously been an orchard. The old apple trees had been preserved, and the garden was really lovely. We had acquired a new family member – a wire-haired terrier called 'Tess', which Olga had been taking for walks because the owners, who lived next door to us in Nursery Close, were at work all day. They ended up by giving her to Olga, as they were really not interested in the poor dog, and probably glad to see her go to a good home. Tess was a nice little dog with a good pedigree. Much more important to us, she had an affectionate nature, apart from when she spotted another dog of which she did not approve, then it was quickly on with her lead and away in the opposite direction. Tess, true to her breed, could be a fighter all right when she chose to be, but generally she was very docile and a good family pet.

We were certainly creatures of habit, for we returned every August for our summer holiday either to Mrs McCarry's bungalow on Hayling Island or to Southsea, meeting up on the beach with all our old friends and enjoying every minute, just as we always had. Our ties to Hampshire and the south coast remained very strong. I think all of us missed the sea at times.

1936 was a very memorable year, or at least, the latter part of it was, for two major events took place which shook the nation. The first, the lesser of the two momentous happenings, was the fire at the Crystal Palace, which destroyed the building completely. I was awakened on the night of November 30th by my mother, who was obviously in a state of great excitement, and probably realising that we were about to witness a piece of history. She said, "You *must* come and see this," and hurried me into the next bedroom where there was a clearer view. We all gathered round the window and gazed in amazement – the whole sky was glowing red and though we were a considerable distance from the fire, we could just see the flickering of flames in the distance. Watching that famous edifice being destroyed before our eyes was an awesome sight. Little did I know then that four years later the sky would be glowing red again, but for a far more sinister reason.

On December 11th the whole country was rocked by the abdication of Edward VIII. We listened incredulously to his speech. Such had been the secrecy surrounding his association with Wallis Simpson that the loss of our popular monarch before he had even been crowned came as a complete shock to everyone. My father, a fan of the Prince of Wales, continued to call him 'the King' till his dying day. We children probably did not realise the seriousness of the event as did the adults, but the playground rang with *'Hark, the herald angels sing: Mrs Simpson's pinched our king'* rather than the more traditional version. We all really hated Mrs Simpson, in spite of the fact that we knew hardly anything about her.

We were all growing up fast; Paul had left Whitgift after matriculating, and was now working for the Railway Passengers' Insurance Company in George Street, Croydon. Poor lad, I'm sure he did not find office work very enthralling, for his heart was really in his music. By then he had become a very good trumpet player, and was a member of a dance band, busy with 'gigs' nearly every night of the week. I would gaze at him in admiration as he prepared to go out, dressed in his smart DJ and white silk scarf. He had started out with an old second-hand brass trumpet, for which he had saved like mad, and then, when he began earning money, he was able to buy a new silver-plated one, which was his pride and joy. Our house was filled with the music of of Nat Gonella, and Paul's friends in the band would often come and rehearse at our house, provided by my mother with endless supplies of coffee. Olga was now at a secretarial college, learning shorthand and typing, and she also was musically inclined. She and a few friends started a small group called 'Ann Kenley and her Silver Serenaders' with Olga at the piano, but I don't think it performed anywhere other than our sitting room! I was coping with obligatory piano lessons with Miss

Dell, in Shirley, but though I passed a few of the lower grades in the Associated Board examinations, I really had minimal talent where the piano was concerned. I do regret this, and my mother was puzzled. Absolutely everyone in her family – and Olga and Paul – could play really well, but not me. Ah, well – maybe other talents would develop later.

As I progressed through the school and reached the age of ten, the scholarship examination loomed. At the most significant stage in our education we had a form master – a Mr Hatton – who during this crucial year was supposed to be preparing us for this important examination and instructing us according to the syllabus, but alas, as it turned out, he was not doing his job at all. In fact, I remember many afternoons spent listening, enthralled and terrified, to the lurid escapades of Conan Doyle's Brigadier Gérard, (which Mr Hatton read with commendable dramatic input) when we should have been preparing for the approaching exam. The class duly sat the scholarship test on the appointed day, and *nobody passed*! That was nothing short of amazing, as there were many bright children there who should have passed with flying colours, and the success rate ought to have been high. What happened after that, I don't know, but we all had to stay on another year in order to take the examination again the following summer. There must have been quite a row, for Mr Hatton disappeared without trace, and we had a new form master, a Mr Larkinson, the next term. He was a strict but wonderful teacher and we all made great progress under his tuition, which produced excellent scholarship successes for the Benson School entrants next time round. I won a place at Coloma – a convent grammar school in Croydon, with an extremely good reputation.

It was August, 1939. I was nearly twelve, and the world was about to change for ever.

'... NO SUCH UNDERTAKING HAS BEEN RECEIVED ...'

Preparations for a possible war with Germany had been going on for some time, but very few people really thought it would happen. On September 1st blackout regulations came into force, and every household had to find some way to ensure that not a chink of light was visible after dark. Blackout material was readily available, so existing curtains were either lined with that, or secondary curtains made. Our house had large bay windows typical of the nineteen-twenties and thirties, and it was quite a problem to ensure that no light escaped down the edges. Sometimes drawing pins had to be used to fasten the curtains to the window frame, and I remember my parents going outside after dark to ensure that no light was visible Some people tacked black paper on to wooden frames which they fitted to the windows, but that involved the boring process of taking them down each day. Car headlamps were covered, and a minimum amount of light was directed downward on to the road through narrow slits. Traffic lights were treated in the same way. Air Raid Wardens became a familiar sight, and an angry shout "Put that light out!" was heard if anyone dared to show the tiniest glimmer – even the lighting of a cigarette outdoors was condemned. If we had for any reason to go out after dark, we would carry a torch, pointed downwards, with the beam partly obscured. We didn't want to be the object of the dreaded 'Put that light out!' reprimand from a warden on duty.

Gas masks had been issued, laughed at and tried on with muffled complaints. "Oh, I couldn't *ever* wear that – I'd rather be gassed!"

we'd complain, tearing off the offending appliance with relief, and gasping for breath. It seemed almost impossible to breathe when wearing the mask – I felt it both claustrophobic and suffocating. However, I suppose we'd have been only too glad of them if the Germans had employed poison gas. We had to take the masks back to a depot soon after they were issued, to have an extra green filter fitted, so I presume a more lethal type of gas had been discovered. As time passed, we became accustomed to carrying gas masks everywhere we went, either in their original cardboard boxes with strings to go over our shoulders, or in fancy cases made to look like handbags – the latter much favoured by many ladies. These were not really approved by the authorities, as it was considered that the gas mask could be damaged in a soft case. Fashion prevailed, however, and cases appeared in all colours and designs, as decorative – if somewhat macabre – accessories.

Some children had already been evacuated to the country, and various instructions given out, but we still thought – at least, we children – that it would all would blow over. After all, hadn't the Prime Minister, Neville Chamberlain, come back from Germany the previous year, waving a piece of paper signed by Adolf Hitler, and declaring that there would be 'peace in our time'? Our parents were no doubt extremely anxious and regarding the ominous events in Europe with much more trepidation than we were. To us, not realising the tragedy that war would bring, the tense atmosphere was strange and exciting. In retrospect, I now realise the anguish which must have been felt by my mother – to have a son of twenty at that dangerous time must have been deeply disturbing. But we children continued our carefree life heedless of the uncertain future which threatened us all. We carried on skipping, chanting the familiar rhymes, playing our favourite games, laughing and joking as usual, oblivious of the fact that already Austria and Czechoslovakia had capitulated to the Nazi jackboot, and that Hitler invaded Poland on September 1st. But our parents continued to listen to every news bulletin and read the daily papers with deepening anxiety.

The storm clouds were gathering in Europe and steadily spreading northwards.

Although talk of war had been in the air for some considerable time, nothing could have prepared us for the impact of that fateful announcement on September 3rd. It was a Sunday, a beautiful late summer's day, and I remember exactly where we all were at that moment of the declaration of war with Germany. Paul was out, as usual, but the rest of us were standing in the breakfast room with the wireless on – an announcement had been given out earlier that an official statement would be made to the nation at eleven fifteen that morning.

Exactly on time the Prime Minister began to speak in his rather clipped, uninspiring voice:

"I am speaking to you from the Cabinet Room at 10 Downing Street. This morning the British Ambassador handed the German Chancellor a final note stating that unless we heard from them that by 11am that they were prepared at once to withdraw their troops from Poland, a state of war would exist between us.

I have to tell you that no such undertaking has been received. Consequently this country is at war with Germany."

The speech continued, and we listened in silence. Just after it ended, there was the most terrifying noise – the air raid siren on the corner of the street started to wail ominously, sounding a warning – were the Germans attacking already? My father shouted, "Put your gas masks on! Take cover!" and he pushed poor Olga into the cupboard under the stairs. "Out of this room – there's too much glass in here!" he ordered, and there *was* indeed a tall glass-fronted dresser and a large window. "Don't be ridiculous!" my mother said, "It's far too soon for anything to happen." and she and I went to the front door and looked up and down the road. Sure enough, the 'All Clear' signal sounded almost at once, and we all breathed a sigh of relief. It had been a false alarm. But the sound of that siren giving the first air raid warning caused a shiver to run down my spine.

With the official declaration of war, the atmosphere of the country changed completely, and everyone became aware of the possible dangers which might lie ahead. Windows of many houses began to display complicated lattice work made from brown paper strips stuck on to the glass. "They look really awful!" commented my mother disapprovingly, and the result did look very strange, but the strips were intended to prevent splinters flying everywhere in the event of the windows being shattered by bomb blast. No doubt they would be very efficient, but the thought of that possibility made us shiver in anticipation of what might lie ahead. We did not have to glue brown paper to our own windows, as we were fortunate to have square leaded lights, and no large panes of glass. Church bells were silenced for the 'duration', only to be rung in the event of a German invasion. The evacuation of children accelerated. Mainline stations were thronged with parties of youngsters, some hardly more than toddlers, waiting to board trains which would convey them to unknown destinations. They clasped an assortment of suitcases, bags and brown paper parcels, and each child wore a label. Mothers stood in unhappy groups, trying to hold back their tears, and harassed teachers tried to keep order. The children were encouraged to sing – probably to give the whole operation a cheerful, holiday atmosphere. I believe one of the favourite songs, of the London evacuees, at least, was 'The Lambeth Walk'. 'Me and My Girl', the show from which that hit number came, had opened at the Victoria Palace in 1937, starring Laurie Lupino Lane, and had a long and successful run. (Ironically I was to appear in the 1984 revival, transferring from the Haymarket Theatre, Leicester, to the Adelphi) We heard that 250,000 children had been evacuated from London alone, and many more from other large cities. There was an air of excitement amongst them to begin with, but it was feared that reaction would set in when night fell and they realised that they were with complete strangers, in unfamiliar surroundings and far from their mothers. There were harrowing tales of the nicer looking children being selected first by their prospective hosts, and the less attractive ones being left until last, with the carers trying desperately to place them. Some people only wanted to take girls, some boys, and this led to siblings being separated against their will in spite of their tearful protestations. How sad that must have been. With all the talk of the intensive bombing which was predicted, my parents wondered if it was wise to keep us at home, so near to London. But to send me away to an unknown destination, labelled like a parcel, to be cared for by strangers, was totally unacceptable to them. So, not willing to have me evacuated from Croydon on the official scheme, my father found out the address of an aunt of a friend of his who lived in the country village of Balcombe, in Sussex. She agreed to take me – Olga, too – and we were hastily despatched to what seemed to us the back of beyond. We arrived at a Victorian terraced house rejoicing in the name 'Calliope' – a curious coincidence, as that was the name of a role I was to play in the Sadler's Wells production of Offenbach's *Orpheus in the Underworld* many years later. Our ancient hostess seemed to live in another age. Unbelievable as it may be now, she had no electricity, and we were given one solitary candle to take upstairs when we went to bed, and that had to last for several nights. Olga and I shared a big brass bed with a feather mattress. Living there was primitive in the extreme. In our bedroom was a marble-topped wash-stand, complete with jug and basin – we had never seen anything like it. The lavatory was outside, and a large china chamber pot, which we regarded with horror, resided under the bed. We were not made at all welcome, and begged our parents to let us come home. After all, no danger had occurred to keep us away. There was absolutely nothing to do; we went for walks – luckily the weather was glorious – as we were not really wanted in the house during the day, except at mealtimes. We used to stand and watch the trains at Balcombe station, wishing with all our hearts that we could jump on one and go home. Though it seemed endless, I suppose our stay in Balcombe only lasted a couple of weeks at the most, for that was the time of the 'phoney war', when absolutely nothing happened at all. Many evacuees returned to London and other big cities, as we did. There is no doubt that for a considerable time we were all lulled into a sense of false security, for things seemed almost normal. I was soon due to start the autumn term at my new school, and I did not want to miss that.

There was my uniform to be bought, and my mother and I pored over the list of things I would need. The usual gym slip, of course, navy piped with royal blue, blue blouses and a school tie; black stockings – how I groaned at that prospect – and a black velour hat with a blue and white hatband, crossing at the front, with a metal badge that bore the motto: '*Laborare est Orare*' (To Work is to Pray). 'What do we wear in the summer?' I asked anxiously, and we glanced down the list. The summer uniform sounded formidable: a royal blue cotton dress with white collar, cuffs and belt, and – wait for it – *grey lisle* stockings! After a lifetime in white ankle socks this sounded dreadful. Even more daunting was the stern ruling that 'all dresses must touch the floor when kneeling'. Goodness, I thought, I'm only going to Coloma to be a pupil, not a *nun!*

Nevertheless I settled into my new school very well, clad in the regulation uniform, to which I soon became resigned, and made friends quickly. Brought up in the Church of England, I was fascinated by the nuns and grew to like them very much, some more than others. I was awed by the crucifixes and holy statues everywhere – the Blessed Virgin Mary, The Sacred Heart, the Infant of Prague, to name but a few. The Roman Catholic atmosphere of the school was all-pervasive, and at that adolescent age, I was very susceptible to its influence, though I must state categorically that at no time was any attempt made to persuade non-Catholic girls into the Roman faith, nor was there ever shown any discrimination against us. I used to love to tiptoe into the chapel, which smelt of furniture polish and incense – I can smell it now. There was such a peaceful atmosphere in there, and I gazed in awe at the statue of the Virgin

Mary, dimly lit by the many candles which burned continuously. Before long I was joining in all the prayers at assembly – I had never heard of the 'Hail Mary' before, but I was soon chanting it along with all the rest. At twelve noon every day the chapel bell would sound the Angelus, and no matter what important work we were engaged in, up we'd all jump for the prayers. Many a boring maths lesson was interrupted in this way, and a welcome respite provided.

Discipline was fairly strict at Coloma. House shoes (black leather with a strap across the instep) must be worn in school, long hair plaited or tied back, and courtesy and good manners shown to the nuns and other teachers at all times. To receive a 'politeness mark' for rudeness was a matter of the greatest seriousness; a 'diligence mark' somewhat less grave. Pupils must never leave the premises without wearing hats and gloves, and behaviour when in school uniform must be impeccable. I sometimes watch the young people of today coming out of school with shirts hanging out, scruffy trainers and even scruffier hair, eating and drinking as they go, and thinking to myself Is this *progress* – am I just behind the times? I wonder. We at least had enormous pride in our school and wanted everyone to know it. Having said that, I recall the suffering of one poor girl who came to school in a dress that was shorter than the regulation length. She was made to stand on a chair in front of the whole class while one of the nuns ripped out the stitches and let down the hem. The offender had to spend the rest of the day with the frayed and uneven hem proclaiming her transgression. Maybe that was discipline taken a little bit *too* far.

The nuns at Coloma, known as 'Ladies of Mary' were all addressed as 'Mother', not 'Sister' as I would have expected. They were clad from head to foot in black, with a broad blue panel down the front of the habit, white wimples and black veils – not at all the sort of relaxed dress worn by nuns today. As they walked along the corridor you could hear the swishing of their long robes and the rattling of their rosaries. One of the girls claimed she had been through the forbidden door into their private quarters, and seen their sleeping accommodation. She whispered to us in great excitement, "What do you *think* – the nuns have *black* sheets!" This was quite obviously untrue, though I'm sure we all believed it at the time.

Next door to us on the right-hand side in Wickham Road lived Mr and Mrs Clark, Marie, (who was about eighteen), Joan, (my age) John, a few years younger, and Bonnie, their black and white terrier. We used to play together quite a lot, in one garden or another. The Clarks had a natty gadget called the 'Kum-Bak' which consisted of two poles about ten feet apart with a string between them. Attached to this in the centre was a tennis ball on strong elastic. This strange contraption ensured that we could have quite a spirited game of tennis without continually lobbing the ball into our neighbours' gardens. Marie 'played' the piano, and I remember my poor mother nearly tearing her hair out at the relentless (and almost unrecognisable, both in time and notation) rendering of Tchaikovsky's 'Valse des Fleurs' which permeated the walls of our sitting room daily. At other times Joan's wheezy wind-up gramophone would play many times a day the latest favourite hit:

> *'There's a grand holiday everywhere,*
> *For the Jones family have a brand new heir,*
> *And he won't be a dud*
> *Or a stck-in-the-mud,*
> *'Cos he's Franklin D Roosevelt Jones!*
> *Yes siree, Yes siree, Yes sireeeeee!'*

But we liked the Clarks very much in spite of these small annoyances and we all got along extremely well.

On the other side of us lived Mr and Mrs Northwood and their dog Gypsy. Mrs N was very elegant, and tied a chiffon scarf round her suspiciously bright red hair when doing the dusting. Their son

Don, who later became a Spitfire pilot, was heavily involved in the Battle of Britain and would ensure that his 'victory roll' – a reckless acrobatic feat performed by many of the pilots at the end of a particularly fierce and successful dogfight – included a very low swoop over our houses. Exciting stuff. He was alleged to have dropped a pair of boots into his mother's garden on one of these occasions.

With the onset of war we were all asked to contribute every bit of scrap metal we could to 'help build Spitfires' or so it was said. A metal dump was established on the corner of the road, close to the air raid siren, and began to fill rapidly with strange bits of metal. Joan and I searched everywhere to find contributions to the dump, which we would hurl on to the heap with a satisfying clatter. "Do you really want this saucepan? Can I have it?" I would ask my mother, selecting what I considered to be a suitable candidate for disposal. "Certainly not!" she would say indignantly, "Goodness knows when we'll be able to get any more." Although shortages of consumer goods had not yet hit the shops, no doubt she was remembering the privations of the first world war, which after all was not so very long ago. Even iron railings began to disappear in aid of the alleged manufacture of aeroplanes, but I cannot imagine an elegant Spitfire being constructed from that disparate mass of rubbish. I think the whole thing was engineered in aid of public morale and to make people think they were 'doing their bit'.

Conscription was to come into effect in October 1939, and Paul, wanting to go into the RAF, decided to volunteer straight away. He was initially sent to Hastings for preliminary training. We missed him terribly at home. All his friends had joined up too, and our house was no longer filled with music and the comings and goings of young people. It seemed very quiet. My mother and I went to Hastings for the day to visit Paul a few weeks later. We arrived at the station where checks were being carried out on visitors, and we could see Paul waving and smiling on the other side of the barrier. "That's my son!" said my mother proudly to the official, whereupon we were waved through. I gazed in admiration at my adored brother, resplendent in his new air force blue uniform, complete with white flash in his forage cap, which denoted his training status. The RAF had commandeered a large modern block of flats right on the sea front, and that was where Paul was billeted – quite a luxurious start. I believe it was called Marine Court, and can only just have been built. We had such a time that day, talking and laughing, hearing about his first impressions of the RAF and the friends he had made, eating candy floss and buying sticks of rock – in fact, all the things that everyone used to do on outings to the seaside. We had a riotous time in the amusement arcade, trying all the unsophisticated machines of those times – rolling pennies down chutes on to lucky squares, playing miniature football, and screaming with laughter as we peered into an ancient device to find out 'What the Butler Saw'. Access to the beach was restricted by barricades of barbed wire, but we didn't care about that, we were enjoying ourselves so much. If only time could stand still, I thought. At last it was time to catch our train home, and we walked sadly back to the station. We could hardly bear to wave to Paul – it was so hard to say goodbye. The war had seemed very far away on that wonderful day.

THE REAL WAR BEGINS

The rest of 1939 passed – for us, at least – fairly uneventfully, but Hitler continued his relentless conquest of Europe and the distance between England and the advancing German troops seemed to diminish daily. But, we children told one another, our forces combined with the French would easily halt their progress, and besides, we were an island. Should the worst come to the worst, we had the Channel between us and the enemy. We watched delightedly as barrage balloons appeared over sensitive areas, and grew quite fond of the great silver things which dominated the skyline. These were either winched up into the air from fixed positions or from RAF trucks which, being mobile, could locate the balloons where they were currently needed. They were attached to extremely strong metal cables, and intended to deter dive bombers or low flying enemy aircraft. Any plane which flew into one of these cables wouldn't have a chance, we were sure.

The Führer was depicted as a figure of fun in cartoons and on posters. Children sang, 'Hitler's barmy, So's his army, Whistle while you work!' to the well-known tune from the recently-released 'Snow White and the Seven Dwarfs', to which we'd all been taken by our parents. We'd goose-step grotesquely around, giving a caricature of the Nazi salute – the potential disasters of war had not registered with us yet – or certainly not as far as we children were concerned .There were no major shortages in the shops yet, and I suppose we were lulled into a false sense of security. Paul came home on leave from time to time, with stories of what he was doing, though of course, only what he was free to tell us. We all became obsessed with an eccentric game of Rummy, which we played on every possible occasion. It usually ended with much shrieking and laughter and tearing of hair. "I'm never playing this again!" the losers would moan bitterly, but we were soon sitting down for the next game. While we were thus engaged, the war with all its potential dangers temporarily receded into the background.

As the old year slipped away and 1940 dawned, we were faced with something quite new – rationing. Ration books had been issued some time previously, but on January 8th they became part of our lives, and we had to become accustomed to a sharp reduction in food consumption. We were required to register with a grocer for butter, bacon and sugar, and the amounts allowed were amazingly small. Two ounces of butter, four ounces of bacon and three of sugar a week seemed seriously inadequate, and we regarded our first rations with grave doubt. My mother devised a way of adding some milk to our small allowance of butter and beating it up in a bowl to increase the volume. It was quite acceptable, and a good thing to do until milk was rationed as well, later on. More commodities would join the restricted list before long. One was meat, which varied in the amount allowed – I remember it being one shilling and two pence-worth per week at one time. Offal and sausages were not rationed, but these gradually became rare treats, often being unavailable, and sometimes even kept 'under the counter' for chosen customers. It was not unknown for younger more glamorous mums to give the butcher the 'glad eye' in the hope that he might slip an odd sausage in with their meat ration. Later, In 1943, even those were rationed. Whale meat began to appear in the shops, but we shuddered and left it there, though some people thought it acceptable. Our mothers became adept at transforming meagre ingredients into satisfying meals, but although missing a ready supply of sweets, cakes and biscuits, I can't ever remember feeling really hungry. Food did tend to become rather monotonous though, with many imported goods impossible to obtain, and strange recipes evolved.

Being an island was all very well in many respects, but much of our food was imported and must be brought into the country by ships. I don't think that we, as children, thought much about this at the time, We merely grumbled when items of food which we took for granted became increasingly unavailable, such as oranges and bananas, not realising that convoys trying to bring us supplies were becoming increasingly at risk from enemy attack, particularly from u-boats. I often think now that inadequate tribute has been paid to the merchant navy, who went through hell to to keep the country from starvation.

School went on as usual, but there were rumours that if and when Croydon came under attack from German bombers, Coloma would relocate to Eastbourne. However, for the moment nothing was happening, and we felt in a kind of limbo. There was rationing, the blackout, children evacuated to the country, though many returned, and not much else. Perhaps the war would be over quite soon, we children thought hopefully, as sweets and chocolate became more difficult to obtain. But plenty was happening in Europe. In April Hitler's army had invaded Norway and Denmark, and on May 10th they entered France. This was uncomfortably close, and tension rose. We felt powerless. Two more momentous events happened on that day: Neville Chamberlain resigned and Winston Churchill became Prime Minister.

Suddenly everything changed. On May 13th Churchill made his first speech in the House of Commons. 'I have nothing to offer but blood, toil, tears and sweat' he said simply, and there was something in that voice – the tone, the inflexions, the *honesty* – that won the nation's immediate support.

The message couldn't have been more sombre, yet it inspired the whole country and gave us the will to fight. Even as a child I realised the importance of his status, and we took him to our hearts. In retrospect I wonder what we as children found so compelling in this elderly, slightly round-shouldered man with his cigar and eccentric siren suit. Of course, it was 'charisma' – a word we'd never heard of in those days. Churchill appealed to everyone, regardless of age or status, and his scornful mispronunciation of the name 'Nazi' (he pronounced it 'Nar<u>z</u>i' and not 'Na<u>tz</u>i') encouraged us to ridicule Hitler and his band of thugs and treat them with the disgust they deserved. "Good old Winnie !" we cheered. Thank God, at last we had a leader. From that moment Neville Chamberlain was consigned to history.

Things were going badly in Europe; we heard on the wireless of the terrible bombing of Belgium and Holland and their subsequent surrender – inexorably the enemy was approaching our coast as the Allies were forced to retreat. In May the majority of the British and French forces were surrounded, and on the 27th 'Operation Dynamo' began – the terrifying rescue of our troops from the beaches of Dunkirk under relentless attacks from Junkers 87 Stuka dive-bombers. We listened to every news bulletin on the wireless with our hearts in our mouths. Several of my schoolmates had fathers, brothers, uncles, cousins involved; their faces were white and strained as we waited for news. As the great rescue effort proceeded, girls would quietly disappear from school for a few days. We knew then that their families had received the fatal telegram. Later they would return, pale and quiet, and the nuns were particularly gentle with them, as we all were. Other girls were luckier as they heard of their relatives' survival – even to be informed that a loved one was seriously wounded was preferable to receiving the worst news of all. Many stories of courage were told. Little ships of every kind, from pleasure steamers to cabin cruisers, helped in the desperate exercise to bring the soldiers back home, sailing to Dunkirk and picking up the men out of the water under severe fire with incredible bravery. We listened to the news and read the papers with horror at the distressing stories of our troops being machine-gunned and dive-bombed by Stukas as they tried to climb aboard the rescue boats. The small craft were often overloaded in their attempt to rescue as many as possible, and some even went back a second time. We were intensely proud when we learned of these tales of courage in the face of such tremendous odds. As a twelve-year-old inspired by a sense of fierce patriotism, I took up my pen to write a poem:

DUNKIRK

They did not flich when Duty bound
Them with his heavy yoke;
They did not quail when forced to fight
Through hell's dark fire and smoke.
Those were the ones who fought for us,
For this, our native land;
Those were the ones who lost their lives
On Dunkirk's yellow sand.

Through ceaseless rain of German bombs
They kept their self control;
For steel can only wound men's flesh
But ne'er can harm his soul.
When British ships to rescue came,
They sent the wounded first;
They lifted them aboard the ships
Mid mad machine gun burst.

But some brave men did not return,
And many died that day;
And many fell as to the ships
They tried to fight their way.
But we will e'er remember them
Who duty did not shirk;
Their names live on through history-
The Heroes of Dunkirk.

Sentimental? Undoubtedly. Patriotic? Certainly. But remember, it was the sincere outpouring of a young girl not yet in her teens, caught up in those extraordinary times and endeavouring to express her feelings at the increasingly terrible events that were unfolding around her.

In recent years I was fascinated to find out that Second Officer Lightoller, survivor of the ill-fated *Titanic*, and long retired from his last position as Commander, had put to sea in his small boat for Dunkirk and rescued a large number of soldiers. He was by no means a young man by then – a great seafarer and a true hero.

The wireless was our vital link with the progress of the war. When the miraculous evacuation of 380,000 troops was completed against tremendous odds on June 4th, Churchill gave his famous 'We shall fight them on the beaches' speech to rally the dispirited people. And it did. We listened to his grave but inspiring words, squared our shoulders and just got on with things. What else could we do? Nobody ever missed a Churchill speech if they could possibly help it. There were other broadcasts that many of us listened to, but these were greeted with derision and probably a few rude noises. They were the pro-Nazi propaganda rantings of William Joyce – alias 'Lord Haw Haw', broadcasting from Hamburg. His drawling sarcastic tones would announce "Germany calling! Germany calling!" and he would proceed to attempt to undermine morale, giving out spurious numbers of British casualties, ships sunk, aircraft shot down. The clever thing was that every now and then he would insert a piece of genuine information into his despicable news bulletin, with the intention of trying to make us wonder whether some of the other announcements might also be true. But we mostly regarded him as a joke, and a traitor to this country. I remember sticking out my tongue at the wireless set during his broadcast, and making other rude signs. Although Joyce was born in Ireland, he held a British passport, and this fact qualified him to be tried in this country after the war for high treason, and executed. Good riddance.

But the news and Lord Haw Haw were by no means the only programmes we listened to on the wireless. Morale had to be kept high and much entertainment was provided to do just that. Variety shows, 'Forces' Favourites' and 'Band Waggon' were programmes not to be missed in our house. Elsie and Doris Waters – ('Gert' and 'Dais'), talking about their husbands Bert and Wally, had us in stitches, Suzette Tarry with her signature tune 'Red Sails in the Sunset' and Jeanne de Casselis as the posh and eccentric 'Mrs Feather' made us laugh till we cried. Then there was Arthur Askey, with 'Stinker' Murdoch in their legendary flat above the BBC, their char, Mrs Bagwash, and her daughter Nausea. What escapades they got up to – we never tired of listening to them. 'Monday Night at Seven' (later 'at Eight') brightened the beginning of the week. I remember the catchy signature tune so well:

'It's Monday Night at Seven – oh, don't you hear the chimes?
We're telling you to take an easy chair,
So settle by the fireside, get out your 'Radio Times'
For 'Monday Night at Seven's on the air'

This was a magazine-type programme which contained Ronnie Waldman's 'Puzzle Corner', Syd Walker's problematic 'What would *you* do, chums?', several comedy spots, singers – Judy Shirley and Anne Lenner, I believe, and of course, music from Charles Shadwell, I think it was, and his orchestra. That was the thing about all those old programmes – there was always a great band involved – sorely missed these days. And every item had its own signature tune, in which we all joined vociferously – Ronnie Waldman's 'Puzzle Corner' for instance:

'Get your pencil and your paper out,
You're the winner if you know about
Who the – what the – where the – why the – when,
Which and wherefore and how – now-
Which and wherefore and how !'

Syd Walker was an rag and bone man from the east end of London, and every Monday he'd tell about someone's problem that he'd encountered, to which he was trying to find a solution. He invariably ended up by saying, 'What would *you* do, chums?' leaving you wondering how on earth to deal with the impossible situation, and coming back at the end of the programme with a miraculous answer. And, talking of comedy shows, I mustn't forget 'ITMA' with Tommy Handley, which must have been one of the most popular ones of all. The cast of extraordinary characters – 'Colonel Chinstrap', the sinister 'Funf', 'Ally Oop' and the charlady, 'Mrs Mopp' with her "Can I do yer now, sir?" which became a national catchphrase, cheered everyone up. These lighthearted distractions took us all away for an hour or two from the grave news in Europe, which is exactly what they were intended to do.

My mother was deep into the afternoon serials on Radio Luxembourg – I remember hearing some of the episodes in the school holidays. There was 'Stella Dallas' and one called – I believe – 'Widow Brown' , which always began with a short 'new readers join here' introduction, indelibly fixed in my memory. It ran as follows: 'Living in the little town of Appleton, young Peggy Jones, a widow in her twenties, ponders long over the question of what she owes to her children and what she owes to herself' – why on earth should I remember that, when I can't recall anything about the actual story? Commercials reigned supreme, too, some dating from before the war, with jingles which we all sang with the radio. There was 'The Beetox Hour' promoting that product, which was a kind of poor man's Bovril – ('Hurrah for Beetox – what a delightful smell !') Cigarette advertising – flourishing then, of course – was prevalent, and *'Mine's a Minor – the best cigarette you can possibly get!'* was one of the most popular jingles. But the 'Ovalteenies' Sunday programme was a real favourite, and badges were issued to all children who joined the club. We didn't like Ovaltine at all, but joined raucously in singing the promotional song:

'We are the Ovalteenies, happy girls and boys,
Make your request, we'll not refuse you,
We are here just to amuse you!
Will you share our songs and stories?
Will you share our joys?
Because we all drink Ovaltine
We're happy girls and boys!' Ugh!

It seems that all sorts of 'nonsense' songs became popular during those war years. They were sung frequently on the wireless, and everyone – from adults to children – joined in with great gusto. One of the early ones – in 1941, I believe, was the 'Hut -Sut Song', or 'Swedish Serenade'. It ran something like this:

'Hut-Sut Rawlson on the rillerah and a brawla, brawla sooit,
Hut-Sut Rawlson on the rillerah and a brawla sooit.
Now, the Rawlson is a Swedish town,
The rillerah is a stream,
The brawla is the boy and girl,
The Hut-Sut is their dream'

At least, in that case the (Swedish) lyrics were translated, and it had a very catchy tune which you couldn't get out of your mind. Some of the other popular numbers were just gibberish – take 'Chickery Chick', for instance!

'Chickery Chick, cha-la, cha-la,
Check-a-la-romey in a bananika,
Bollika Wollika, can't you see
Chickery Chick is me!'

There were many others, of course – *'Tisket, A-Tasket, a green and yellow basket'* for instance, and that old favourite *'Mairzy doats and dozey doats and liddle lamzy divey'* (Mares eat oats and does eat oats and little lambs eat ivy). We children loved them all, and rattled them off at the tops of our voices. It is just as well that we had such distractions, for the war news was becoming ever more serious.

On June 9th there was a major offensive on Paris, on the 14th the German army entered the city, and we heard that infamous Nazi flags bearing the hated swastika were appearing everywhere, draped on public buildings, and even over the Arc de Tromphe. On the 22nd the French surrendered and the war in Europe was over. Regulations tightened in this country and we braced ourselves for a possible invasion. After all, there were only twenty or so miles between us and the French coast – could we possibly prevent it? Food rationing was extended and by July tea and cooking fat were included. My mother's face dropped a mile when she heard that we were to be allowed three ounces of tea per person per week. However, we managed. We heard that some people were drying the used tea leaves and infusing them again. This must have produced a very insipid brew – still, I suppose it was better than nothing. I remember the pallid packets of unappetising margarine at four pence-halfpenny for half-a-pound – but we were glad to have it. Some people mixed it with butter, but we never did. We enjoyed the tiny amount of butter allowed, then shrugged our shoulders and finished the week on 'marge'. Later, for tinned goods and preserves we had coupons known as 'points' but the variety of items in this category was becoming increasingly limited. At one stage each person was allowed one egg per week. We were beginning to feel the pinch.

Paul was sent up to Prestwick for further training, so didn't get home on leave so often. He was very much missed. We received a beautiful tartan tea cosy adorned with a sprig of white heather as a souvenir from Scotland; I have it still. As was customary, he made a monthly allowance to my mother from his RAF pay, and in his letter telling her of this, said, 'and give a couple of bob to Cynth – she's always short of money!' This was typical of him; even as a child, I was very touched. He was to train to be an observer, or navigator and bomb-aimer as it became known, which must have filled my mother with anxiety, though she said nothing. As a twelve-year-old, I merely felt excited and proud to think he would be flying before long.

Coloma was relocating to Eastbourne as had been expected, to share premises and facilities with the local High School – an unfortunate decision as it turned out, for the south coast was to become a very dangerous area. I heard that later on they had to move again, this time to Wales. School holidays began in July, so with the uncertainty of the progress of the war, there was nothing much that could be done about my schooling until September. There was also a possibility of my father's transfer to Birmingham in the near future, so the question of my education when the next school year began remained unresolved. And then the air raids started. We know now that Hitler had been poised to launch his 'Operation Sealion' which meant a full-scale assault along several miles of the south coast, followed by invasion. He was advised to postpone this action in order to give the Luftwaffe the chance to destroy the RAF on the ground and in the air and so prevent their attacking the vulnerable invading forces as they crossed the channel. This was fortunate for us, but a bad miscalculation on his part, for he had not reckoned on the dogged determination of the RAF or the power of our Spitfires and Hurricanes, and the men who flew them.

IS IT ONE OF OURS?

Shirley was a dangerous place to be in the summer of 1940. We were in a very vulnerable position, for Croydon Aerodrome, where Hurricane and Spitfire squadrons were now stationed, was only a few miles away, as were the famous Biggin Hill and Kenley airfields. As Hitler's object was to destroy as many British aircraft on the ground as possible, we were in the middle of some prime targets. And not only was the RAF the object of attack, but the many factories in and around Croydon attracted the Luftwaffe's attention. These were now producing munitions and aircraft parts and were also on Hitler's list for destruction.

I was glad it was holiday time and I didn't to have to get up early and go to school when the interminable night raids began – that would have been really hard. Yawning our way through lessons that failed to have any impact on account of the sheer exhaustion of both pupils and teachers would have been counter-productive. We snatched a few hours' sleep whenever possible, waking with a start to what was becoming a very regular sound. The wailing of the siren became a familiar interruption to our day. We would hear the telephone bell ring in the police box on the corner, and we knew that we must stand by, for if it rang a second time the siren would give the warning to take cover, as enemy aircraft were approaching. That ominous wailing was really an awesome sound; even after all these years I have only to hear an air raid siren in an old wartime film and a shiver runs down my spine. It immediately evokes the atmosphere of those extraordinary times – feelings of dread, yet tinged with excitement, and the camaraderie of both neighbours and complete strangers as we hurried into the shelter together. There were many jokes, of course – mainly about Hitler or Goering, some fairly rude, and all calculated to raise our spirits and morale. If we risked taking the bus for a quick shopping trip to Croydon, and there was suddenly an air raid warning, we'd have to find the nearest shelter there. Many of these were under ground, which I found unpleasantly claustrophobic. During those days of frequent raids it was better not to be far from home, and the shops in Shirley provided pretty well all we really needed. One morning Olga was taking Tess for a walk when the sound of approaching machine gun fire made her leap under a hedge, dragging the dog with her as a stray Stuka roared by, presumably on its way back from Biggin Hill. All the other people in the street had taken similar action, and everyone was badly shaken by the experience. Olga arrived home trembling and terrified. What justification could there possibly be for targeting innocent civilians in this way? And what devilish mind had ordered the installation of a screaming siren on the Stuka to strike terror into the victims as they were dive-bombed? We hated Hitler more than ever – if that were possible.

Some of my friends had Anderson shelters in their gardens, constructed by their fathers. These were made from sheets of corrugated iron, bolted together overhead, another sheet (with an entrance) for the front, and one for the back They measured six feet by four feet six inches, and were reckoned to accommodate six people – obviously a tight squeeze. A suitably sized hole had to be dug for these shelters, so they were largely below ground, often with turves laid over the roofs, and consequently largely camouflaged. Some keen gardeners grew flowers or even vegetables on top of their Anderson. There were two or three steps down into the interior, which was usually damp, dismal and full of spiders and in very wet weather they could become flooded, which was a definite disadvantage. But people made them as comfortable as they could, with makeshift bunks, cushions and blankets, and of course a supply of books and crosswords. Candles provided meagre light during a night raid, and torches were at the ready, carefully shielded to supress any glimmer which might call forth the dreaded "Put that light out!" from a passing warden. Oil lamps were frowned upon, as they posed a fire risk in such a confined space. Thermos flasks of tea and tins of biscuits were an essential part of the equipment needed to sit through an air raid, night or day. There is no doubt that Anderson shelters saved many lives, though they obviously could not have survived a direct hit.

We didn't have an Anderson, so when the siren sounded we would gather up anything we needed and go across the road to take cover in a large surface shelter, which was conveniently opposite our house. This was a rectangular structure, with walls several bricks thick, a concrete floor and a reinforced concrete roof. We told each other we'd be perfectly safe there, though in actual fact, as with the Anderson, a direct hit would have completely flattened the shelter. However, it provided good protection from blast, flying glass splinters and shrapnel, and to be with other people was reassuring. It was pretty comfortless, with wooden seats round the walls – not much fun if you'd been hauled out of a comfortable bed, fast asleep, wrapped in your dressing gown and a blanket, and rushed to this inhospitable refuge for goodness knows how long. Or maybe you were just stepping into a lovely hot bath (only *five* inches of water, remember) and had to pull out the plug furiously, cursing Hitler and his gang, and hurry across the road instead. Night time was the worst; everyone was tired – there had probably been several raids already during the day, and all you longed for was an interrupted night's sleep. We welcomed rainy, misty days and nights, as the Luftwaffe gave us a rest during such weather conditions, but the summer of 1940 seemed to be an unusually fine one. There were days when the 'all clear' (a long, even note on the siren) sounded the end of an 'alert', only to be followed shortly afterwards by yet another warning, and this went on throughout the day – and sometimes the night as well. You'd probably only just put the kettle on, and there it was again. These warnings were not always followed by an actual raid – they meant that enemy aircraft were approaching in our direction. There were many airfields in the south east and Croydon was not always the target, though during August Biggin Hill was bombed constantly. But the signal to take cover was certainly not to be ignored, as very often the distinctive sound of German aircraft could be heard approaching soon after the siren sounded, followed by the frightening noise of bombs exploding, sometimes uncomfortably near. There was no doubt that the German bombers sounded completely different from our own; the engines produced a regular, throbbing note which we could easily identify. During the day we would hear the comforting sound of the Merlin engines of our Spitfires and Hurricanes as they moved in to attack, and this always provoked a cheer from the occupants of the shelter.

I think night raids were the worst. Not being able to go to bed – a novelty at first for us children – became very trying, and in the darkness the roar of the bombers seemed more menacing as they advanced relentlessly, regardless of the searchlights that criss-crossed the night sky. In those early stages of the war there were no night fighters to deter them. A mobile anti-aircraft gun was stationed in Wickham Road and would tear up and down firing with deafening regularity. I don't suppose it achieved very much, but we felt we were being protected. And of course there was plenty of shrapnel to find next day – we children competed with one another to find the largest or most interesting piece. Some of us had quite a collection.

What a motley crew assembled each night in the shelter! The Clark family from next door were there, of course, with Bonnie the dog. Pets could not be left alone in the house to endure the noise of the raid, terrified and vulnerable, so they accompanied their owners as part of the family. Mrs Clark, in her pink hairnet, was laden with so many supplies that you would have thought she was there for the 'duration'. Mr Clark either retired behind his newspaper, reading out selected reports on the progress of the war

The Clark family – drawn in the shelter during an air raid, August 1940

to anyone who would listen, or wandered up and down. Marie was usually to be seen in curlers, partly concealed by a turban, cream on her face, painting her nails and reading 'Red Letter' or some similar magazine. Joan and I usually got together with drawing books and crayons, sometimes producing awful pictures of fellow occupants of the shelter. This caused much giggling and drew reprimands from our mothers, concerned that some folk were trying to get some sleep, though how on earth they could with all that racket going on outside, goodness knows. Olga was always knitting – in fact she knitted her way right through the war, which proved very useful for all of us. Tess, our dog, sat by her, under the seat, for she was terrified by the noise. We knew most of the other occupants by sight, if not by name. There was Mrs Bowman from the house on the corner, who chain-smoked, was thin as a rake and had the

Typical scene in the air raid shelter with the neighbours, 1940

most dreadful hacking cough. "I'm sure she's got TB," my mother whispered darkly to Mrs Clark. A very fat, rubicund gentleman and his diminutive wife, Mr and Mrs Humphreys, were frequent occupants of the shelter. Mr H spent the whole of every air raid pacing up and down while his small wife sat nervously in a corner. If Joan, John and I indulged in any physical activity, a rather posh lady – we weren't sure where she lived, but she was a shelter regular – would glare at us and complain, 'What a dust! What a dust!" which prompted our mothers to tell us to sit still. We called her the 'Dusty Lady' for the want of any known identity, and she featured frequently – in most unflattering guise – in our cartoons.

This all sounds quite a lot of fun, but there were many times when the menacing drone of enemy aircraft was right overhead, and explosions dangerously close. At those times the shelter became very quiet, the atmosphere tense until the danger had for the moment passed, then someone would say, laughing nervously, "Phew – that was close!" and everyone would relax temporarily, relieved that we were all still in one piece.

All sorts of garments were worn in the shelter, depending on whether you had actually got to bed before the siren went, in which case you might have to appear in a dressing gown, hastily draped in a blanket. Or you might have had time to dress for the occasion, maybe even in a smart 'siren suit'. This was a cosy one-piece garment which zipped up the front, with a hood, worn with great aplomb by Churchill, and very popular. I remember wearing a cut-down pair of trousers of Paul's and one of his pullovers, for although it was summer, the shelter tended to be fairly cool after dark. One particular night the raid was intense, and everyone was feeling very weary after a disrupted day. My mother and Mrs Clark had spread a blanket and pillows on the floor and persuaded Joan and me to lie down and try to get some rest. What a hope! The noise was intense – the dull thud of bombs and the racket of anti-aircraft guns was deafening. In the middle of all this the conductor and driver of a 194 bus from Croydon came in with a few of their passengers – they had decided it was too risky to attempt to continue their journey to West Wickham, and they'd better take cover. They were horrified when they saw us children lying on the concrete floor. "That won't do," said the cheery driver, and he disappeared with his mate back out into the inferno, returning in a couple of minutes with some seat cushions from the bus. These made us a most comfortable bed for the rest of the raid – and it was a long one. There were many acts of kindness like that during the war, but that incident is one that I particularly remember.

We heard frequently from Paul, who was concerned about our safety, having heard about the intensive attacks in the Croydon area, but we reassured him that we were coping well. He started flying in August, first in a Fokker plane, then in an Anson, training in navigation, but would not become fully operational for several months. He seemed to enjoy what he was doing, and laughed away my mother's worries; that was always his way, of course.

The period from July 10th to October 31st is now referred to as the 'Battle of Britain', and to those of us who braved the peril, ignored the warning to 'take cover' and stood in our gardens watching the conflict in the skies above, this is a very apt title. I feel proud to have witnessed what later turned out to be a turning point in the war, for so effective were our fighters that by the end of that summer of 1940 Hitler had abandoned 'Operation Sealion' – the invasion of Great Britain. Just as the RAF's resources were at breaking point there was an unexpected breathing space.

Any fear we might have felt was outweighed by excitement as we watched, enthralled. Day after day the enemy bombers came to attack – Dorniers, Heinkels and the dreaded Junkers 87s – or 'Stukas', accompanied by their highly efficient Messerscmitt 109 fighters. Every time they were met by our Spitfires and Hurricanes from Biggin Hill, Croydon and Kenley. We watched spellbound as countless 'dog fights' took place overhead. The blue summer sky was patterned with thin white vapour trails as the fighters dived and manoeuvred high above. Sometimes a scrapping pair would scream down over the houses quite low, and we would shout and cheer, oblivious of the potential danger to ourselves – this was history in the making, and we wanted to be part of it. I can hear the sound of those Merlin engines to this day, and it never occurred to me at the age of twelve that any of our own fighters could possibly be shot down. They were far superior to any of the German planes – I knew that. But the loss of our pilots and aircraft during those crucial weeks was dangerously high – we know that now, though we were told little of this at the time. The beautiful lines of the Spitfire, with its eliptical wings, caught my imagination, though actually the more workmanlike and less glamorous Hurricane shot down more German aircraft. But I loved them both. What I did not appreciate then was the weariness of those overworked pilots, who barely had time to touch down and refuel before they were back in the air again. If they had half an hour to relax between raids they were lucky indeed, for the call to 'scramble' again would often come before they even had time to drink a cup of tea. The loss of life was, inevitably, severe, and experienced fighter pilots were at a premium. Newly qualified young men with only a few hours flying experience found themselves thrown into this furious battle, and for some it was their first – and last – sortie. We were unaware of this at the time – to us every one of those fighter pilots was an ace.

What we loved most of all were the wonderful 'victory rolls' performed by the Spitfires and Hurricanes as the Luftwaffe eventually turned back. Some of the planes gave amazing displays, and flew so low that we would wave wildly in the hope that the pilots would see us. My youthful heart nearly burst with pride at their exploits. How could we not win a war, with men like these ruling our skies? I thought. Needless to say, those of us watching all this ought to have been safely in the shelter – but I would not have missed any of it for all the world.

WE MOVE AGAIN

My father had, as expected, been transferred to Birmingham, and was anxious for us, still braving the air raids. Amongst my mother's keepsakes I found a dog-eared letter I had sent to my father. There is no date on it, but it was obviously written at the time of the continual bombing of the airfields in late 1940. It has a sketch at the top right hand side showing a man in action with a spade, entitled 'this is you covering up the incendiary bomb' so apparently my father had been involved in some incident of that kind up in Birmingham. At the other side is a note saying 'I wear Paul's trousers in the shelter at night !!' The rest is as follows:

Dear Daddy,

We are just waiting for the sirens to go. We have had 2 raids today (Tues). Please put a letter in for me next time you write. It is a quarter to ten and I am going to try & get a bit of rest.

I am not afraid of the dirty old Gerries, we have some fun in the shelter, please send some chocolate as soon as you can. (all makes acceptable)

I really must go now.

Much love from

X X X X Cynthia

P.S.

We have got 2 batteries for our torches.

It seems that batteries must already have been in short supply by 1940 – not surprising, as everybody would have needed them to see their way to various shelters during night raids. It was obviously a great achievement to obtain *two!* Another short note reads:

Dear Daddy,

We are still having plenty of air raids. Yesterday we had 5. I think I've got a cold through sleeping on the floor.

Last night a bomb whistled right down over our house, and I thought it was the end!

Please write to me soon

Much love from Cynthia

This is followed by a very creditable drawing of a Spitfire. From the text of the letter I don't seem to be unduly upset by the near miss!

My father was trying hard to find suitable accommodation for us fairly convenient for his work, not in the city, which might soon become as dangerous as Croydon, but some distance outside, in a more rural environment. He was not finding it easy, for people were leaving London and the south east for less vulnerable areas, and houses and flats to let were at a premium. Finally he decided that Leamington Spa, about twenty miles or so from Birmingham, might be suitable, and he found a furnished flat there which would provide a base from which we could continue looking for something more suitable.

It was quite a wrench to leave Shirley, our friends – even the air raids, and the daily sight of the Spitfires and Hurricanes that patrolled constantly overhead. My drawing books were full of coloured sketches of these planes, with raids and dogfights pictured vividly – and it was always the German bombers and ME 109s being shot down with smoke pouring from their tails! It was strange to think of living in the midlands – would there be air raids up there, I wondered – and what would my new school would be like? Our furniture had to go into storage for the time being, and I remember the last night we spent in Shirley – our house was empty, and we were not to leave until the next day. Kind Mrs Clark offered us the hospitality of her house, and we spent that night – with the usual air raid – next door. The Clarks had acquired a Morrison shelter, and we children slept in there – I can't remember what the adults did, but nobody went across the road when the siren sounded. The Morrison shelter was quite new; people were getting tired of the damp old Andersons, so this latest structure was a large heavy steel affair made for indoor use. It was tremendously strong, made to withstand the impact of heavy debris. It looked rather like a cage, would sleep about four people (if they were on intimate terms!), and could be disguised as a dining table, with a nice table cloth and possibly a vase of flowers when not in use! That night was the only time I experienced one of these things, and I was not very impressed; it was terribly stuffy and rather claustrophobic.

So it was off to Leamington the next day, and after a fond farewell to the Clarks, we set out. Our journey involved taking a train to Victoria, the underground to Paddington, then a Great Western train to our final destination, so we saw little of any bomb damage. In any case, the heaviest of the attacks on London itself occurred during the following year. We were met by my father at Leamington and taken by taxi to Bushbury Lodge, 45 Willes Road, where we were to spend the next few weeks. Our dear wire-haired terrier, Tess, had departed this life at the venerable age of fifteen, but I quickly made friends with Patsy, the elderly spaniel, who belonged to Mrs Hancox, our new landlady. Bushbury Lodge was a large detached early Victorian house in attractive gardens, and we were shown into some very spacious, pleasant rooms with high ceilings. But letting a flat was not the only source of income enjoyed by the owners. We soon found out that our landlady's son ran the Eric Hancox School of Dancing on the premises, and there was a lovely big studio with polished wooden floor where classes were held. This intrigued me greatly, and I soon made friends with Eric, whom I thought to be the epitome of sophistication. I suppose he was about forty, very elegant, rather flamboyant, and a beautiful ballroom dancer. I realise in retrospect that he was extremely kind and patient with the inquisitive thirteen-year-old girl, who often visited him in his studio, asked him endless questions and hung on his every word. He arranged for me to have ballet lessons with one of his star pupils, Pamela Devis, who later became a west end choreographer and ran a troupe of dancers. Perhaps the germ of a future stage career was planted then – who knows?

We explored the attractive spa town of Leamington with curiosity. It was completely different from anything we had known before – Portsmouth was a naval town, adjacent to Southsea, which was a holiday resort. There were some attractive buildings and pleasant parks, and of course – the sea. Croydon was at that time a sizeable town with a busy shopping centre, and Shirley, where we lived, had an almost village-like in atmosphere, in spite of considerable residential development in the twenties and thirties. Royal Leamington Spa was another kettle of fish altogether, with its broad tree-lined streets and Regency houses of great architectural beauty. The Parade – the main thoroughfare – was a wide, gracious street which ran right up through the town, culminating at the top with Christ Church, long since demolished. Many high-class shops were situated there, and must have been impressive in pre-war years, but when we arrived in Leamington in late 1940, these establishments were just beginning to feel the approaching austerity which the privations of war would inflict. However, the dilapidation and general shabbiness which were to affect all these attractive buildings in later years had scarcely begun. There were several department stores – Bobby's, the first shop on the left past the Pump Room Gardens, in a prime position; Woodwards, on the corner of Regent street; a little farther up was a wonderful emporium called Burgis and Colbourne – of which more, later, and a rather cheaper kind of store – Grey's, near Warwick Street. Even in those times Bobby's had beautiful window displays and was a very elegant store. Woodward's was a more homely type of place, and Grey's, with its many bargains and more inexpensive

An ordinary family: l to r: Paul, me, Olga, 1931

Miss Whittle's 'Dainty Dots' 1925 (Olga c)

...and in a starring role 1927

My mother 1929

Paul and me 1929

The latest in beachwear!
Southsea 1930

Wimborne Road School netball team (Olga c.) 1930

My class at the Benson School 1937 (me - 3rd from r, seated)

First stage appearance: a Bee in Benson School play 1937

Leading role- 'Lady Ombersley', 1938

Paul with his new trumpet, 1938

A visit to Hastings, where Paul was training in the RAF 1939 (note gas masks)

Olga with Paul, now operational as navigator/bomb aimer on Wellingtons 1941

Paul and crew before raid on Düsseldorf 1941

Paul (2nd r) with crew, Egypt 1941 (photo: Steve Challen)

Paul (l) with the ill-fated Liberator, Egypt 1942

Nearly grown-up - with friend June and two young farmers! 1945

Mother with Nell and unexpected puppies, 1944

goods was a useful addition. The lower end of the Parade where the Pump Room and the beautiful Jephson Gardens were situated became Victoria Terrace, which led into Bath Street. Here were many smaller shops and another long-established department store, E. Francis & Sons Ltd. Even for those days this was a very dignified and somewhat old-fashioned family-run emporium, with many departments selling good quality merchandise from ladies' corsets to millinery. In the children's section you could buy Chilprufe vests and Peter Pan liberty bodices, tried and trusted undergarments which many of us had worn when we were small.

As we became more acquainted with Leamington we began to like our new town and to feel more settled. There were important matters to be attended to, such as the resumption of my education and I was fortunate to be accepted by a very good grammar school, Leamington College for Girls. This was housed in a large, rather ugly red brick Edwardian building to which I would walk every day – down the Parade, through the Pump Room Gardens, and across the little bridge over the river Leam, for by this time we had moved to a slightly ramshackle and draughty flat on the Parade itself. We didn't like the flat much – it was certainly not what we had been used to, but there was no choice – there was absolutely nothing else to be had. As the agent said, "Don't forget there's a war on!" a saying we were all to hear ad nauseam as things steadily got worse. At least we had a big sunny balcony at the front, where we could sit, and from which we could watch anything that might be happening. The flat was on the first floor of a Regency building which must once have been rather splendid, but the ground floor was now a shop which dealt in agricultural supplies.

One night – it was November 14th – the siren sounded, and for a moment we all thought we were back in Shirley, as we heard the unmistakable throbbing note of German bombers. "I thought we'd finished with all that – what can they be after?" said my mother, "It *can't* be Leamington, surely?" We had no air raid shelter, so stayed where we were. Wave after wave of aircraft passed overhead, on their way to some target or other, and we watched the searchlights as they raked the sky. When we heard the distant thudding of bombs – a familiar sound to us – we went down into the main hall and called to a passing air raid warden to see if he had any information. "It's Coventry," he shouted, "And there are hundreds of 'em! You'd better take cover – we may get a few stray bombs here on their way back," and he disappeared into the darkness. Coventry was a bare ten miles away, and we could see a faint red glow in the sky, which grew brighter as the night wore on. There were of course many munition and aircraft parts factories there, but this raid was evidently geared to more than just that. That disastrous air raid lasted for eleven hours.

We heard next day that the whole of the centre of the city had been destroyed, including the beautiful cathedral, and more than three hundred civilians killed. Apparently five hundred bombers had attacked the city, carrying five hundred tons of high explosives and nearly nine hundred incendiaries. It was a massive raid, not only on legitimate targets, but on the citizens themselves, and aimed to terrorise and destroy morale. Refugees streamed into Leamington and were given shelter, in church halls and other large buildings and in people's homes. It was a dreadful night – we brewed tea incessantly in spite of the rationing – it was essential. And sure enough, as the warden suggested, a series of deafening explosions occurred much later when some surplus bombs were dropped on Leamington as the Luftwaffe made its way home. One of the loudest more or less destroyed Lipton's store farther down the Parade, but uncomfortably close to us. A section of glass blew out of one of our windows, to be replaced by a piece of board for 'the duration' – we just couldn't get any replacement glass, nor anyone to fix it. Luckily it was usually partially hidden by the curtain. There were a number of casualties – very few – but each one a terrible tragedy to the family concerned.

But life went on; I started at my new school, my father travelled to Birmingham every day, and Olga took a post with the Inland

Revenue in a pleasant office farther down the Parade. She was to remain with the civil service for the rest of her working life, which, though it does not sound wildly exciting, involved her being sent immediately after the war with the Allied Control Commission to Vienna and Rome, where she had a wonderful time. During the war years she had to take turns fire-watching overnight on the roof of the Regent Hotel, and would depart on the evenings when she was on duty with blanket, warm clothes – and, of course, a flask of tea. I don't know what good she would have been in the event of an incident, as she was very frightened during air raids – but maybe she would have risen to the occasion when the time came. My mother was busy adapting curtains for the flat – luckily there were substantial interior shutters, so blackout was no problem. Also there was the business of registering with a grocer and butcher. One advantage of our situation was that we were at the centre of everything. We chose a butcher quite near where we lived, and a rather rather old-fashioned grocer in Regent Street, half way down the Parade. This grocery establishment was ruled over by the owner, elderly Mr Empson, who sat at a high desk just inside the door, with a thick ledger in front of him, and ruled his kingdom with a rod of iron. He would look over his glasses when the shop doorbell rang and a customer entered, and greeted every one with a courteous 'Good morning', and a comment about the weather or the progress of the war. We were served by his right-hand man, the obsequious Mr Osbourne, in his spotless white apron, who attended to our rations each week. He would meticulously weigh out our pitiful allowance of butter, and mould it into a neat little block with the practised flourish of a pair of wooden butter pats, exercising just as much care as if he were shaping a pound of best dairy butter for an exhibition. Ration books were examined and marked with an indelible stamp, cancelling out allowances for that week. Tea and sugar was weighed and packed into blue paper bags, bacon and cheese wrapped in greaseproof paper. Small quantities of goods which were as yet unrationed, such as biscuits, were carefully wrapped up, and finally everything was packed into my mother's shopping basket, whereupon we were shown out of the shop with old-fashioned ceremony.

Delivery services were few and far between during the war – many errand boys had been called up or directed into factories. Shopping at Mr Empson's emporium was quite an experience. It was not the same at the butcher, who had moved with the times, and was more down to earth. We collected our meagre amount of meat, plus some offal – if available, and maybe even a couple of sausages if we were lucky – this would be a typical weekly allowance. Much ingenuity was required to make these minimal ingredients into tasty and satisfying meals. Paul would come home on leave occasionally, bringing with him an emergency ration card, which helped with supplies. We were always thrilled to see him, and he certainly brightened the increasing drabness of our lives.

The headmistress of my new school, Leamington College for Girls, was Mrs Anger – an unfortunate name which did not suit her in the least. My mother consulted her on the problem of school uniform. Buying another outfit so soon after the expensive one recently purchased for Coloma seemed an unnecessary extravagance in wartime, and Mrs A agreed that I should continue wearing the latter until I grew out of it, which probably would not be all that long. Rather a pity, as the straight, unpleated air force blue tunics and buff V-neck blouses worn by the girls of Leamington College seemed both attractive and sensible. However, I could see the wisdom of continuing to wear my Coloma uniform for the time being in the light of the current clothing situation, which would probably worsen as the war proceeded. Besides, it had cost my parents a lot of money. There was a thriving market in second-hand school uniform run by the mothers; girls grew out of clothes so fast that they were by no means worn out, and could be sold on to others. No black stockings, either! We were allowed to wear socks or beige stockings, which was quite a relief. Our school badges bore the motto: *Sola Bona Quae Honesta*, which, loosely translated means 'Those things alone are good which are honest'.

I was put into Form IVL, which stood for 'Latin', of which I knew nothing – I should have some catching up to do. We were taught this subject by Miss Hickling, a 'jolly hockey stick' type, enthusiastic about Latin, and keen to pass her love of it on to her pupils. To my surprise, I took to it very quickly. It seemed such a tidy, logical sort of language, and our text book, 'Latin for Today' somehow managed to be very interesting. When Miss Hickling entered the classroom she would say, "Salvete, Discipulae" and we would answer, "Salve Magistra," whereupon we would sit down and open our books.

"Discipulae, picturam spectate," ordered Miss H, and we obediently studied the illustration and the chapter indicated. The book dealt with an ordinary Roman family, their house, their games, pets, how they lived and what they ate. They seemed normal enough sort of people, so we could relate to them and consequently the story held our interest. There was very little about cohorts, legions marching to the ramparts, battles, swords and shields, which usually feature in Latin textbooks. The characters in the book were real to us, and therefore we wanted to know more about them.

French, taught by Mrs Hain, was a favourite subject. I had received a very good grounding in this at Coloma, so got on quickly, and with considerable enjoyment. Our text book, 'Apprenons le Francais!' (which I still possess) was an account of the life of the Laborde family, and we followed their adventures with considerable interest. They indulged in all sorts of useful activities, knowledge of which might prove useful when we visited France at some future date, whenever that might be! Not that any of us, in the present climate, could imagine ever going there, for the situation in Europe was steadily worsening, and any prospect of foreign travel simply didn't exist. On account of the increasing scarcity of paper and publishing restraints, text books were passed down at the end of the school year to the next pupils to need them. Originally purchased new, the price was then reduced for each new owner, and they thus were re-cycled until they were falling to bits. . My French book, published in 1938, is inscribed with the names of two previous owners: Alice McGlasson and Blanka M. Stranska, and when it was handed down to me, it cost one shilling and sixpence. We were also constantly reminded that we must be economical with our exercise books; narrower margins were ordered, and every line was to be filled, no space wasted, pencils to be used right to the end. Austerity was beginning to bite.

WARTIME WINTER

We heard that Paul had passed his observer's, bombing and gunnery courses in November and had flown in a Whitley – we saw these planes fly over from time to time and thought of him. He still had several months of flying training to do before becoming operational. I'm sure my mother was relieved at that, and hoped against hope that the war might be over by then, though it certainly didn't look like it. My father brought home aircraft recognition manuals from his office and I pored over them, memorising the every detail of both English and German aircraft, determined to recognise every one I saw. I remember the square outlines of the Armstrong Whitworth Whitley, and the thin fuselage of the Handley Page Hampden – known, I believe, as the 'frying pan'. Then there was the distinctive engine sound and shape of the Vickers Armstrong Wellington, a plane that was to mean a great deal to us in the future. Recognising Spitfires and Hurricanes was second nature to me, and I was pleased that we still saw quite a few of these, as there were fighter stations at Gaydon and Wellesbourne, not far away. All details of Dorniers, Heinkels, and of course the evil Junkers 87 dive bomber, or 'Stuka', (which was fitted with a screaming siren, used to terrify civilian targets) were carefully studied and memorised.

We felt the hardships of war much more in the winter, as heating was at a minimum, both at school and at home. We just had an open fire in our sitting room and relied on a succession of Valor oil heaters for bedrooms – that is, when paraffin was available. This was sold in the street from a small truck; the driver would ring a bell and you'd hurry out with your gallon can, which he would fill from a tap on the large tank. I used to lie in bed and look at the pattern the stove made on the ceiling before drifting off to sleep, then my mother would creep in and take the Valor away for a turn in her room. Thick nighties and bedsocks were essential – it was either that or freeze. The bedroom I shared with Olga had French windows on to the balcony, and I remember ice forming on the *inside* of the windows during really cold spells. At school we kept our coats on in class, and I wore knitted mittens to try to ward off chilblains – unsuccessfully. My fingers were so swollen that at times it became difficult to hold a pen. I had never experienced such extreme cold. Never mind any thoughts of pretty underwear, even if you could get it, or were prepared to waste carefully-hoarded coupons on it. Woollen vests – sometimes hand-knitted – were the order of the day. Would we ever feel warm again, I wondered. I couldn't imagine it. Sometimes we were sent out into the playground to jump about to try and thaw out. Concentration on lessons was hard to maintain when you felt you were freezing. Skipping was a good way to keep the circulation going, even though we may have considered ourselves too grown-up for such childish activities. There was no question of closing the school for lack of heating when snow was on the ground. We trudged doggedly through all weathers in our wartime winter coats and wellies, stamping the snow off our frozen feet at the school door, glad to get in out of the intense cold, though sometimes it was little better in the classrooms. Knitted gloves were dried on the radiators – if they were warm – and they weren't always, on account of fuel shortages; boots put to drip in the cloakroom and plimsolls (or 'pumps' as they were called) changed into for class. There's no doubt about it – we were tough in those days. There was no other option. You didn't stay away from school unless you were genuinely ill.

School was one of the good things, though. As the new term began in January 1941 we began to look forward to the spring. I made a lot of new friends and enjoyed most subjects – except maths, geography and history. Whether it was the subjects themselves or the mistresses teaching them that failed to arouse my enthusiasm, I don't know, but it was Art, French, Latin and English which I liked best. Biology too, taught by Miss Ford, was interesting, though dissecting rats reeking of formalin and measuring their intestines I found less attractive. The reproductive organs of a frog did not impress me much, either. I once surreptitiously once threw a kidney across the room at a another girl when Miss Ford's back was turned, without her noticing, though she didn't miss much as a rule. History seemed to be merely a string of dates, politics, wars and sagas of religious strife, when it should have been fascinating – knowing that the Congress of Vienna took place in 1815 (a fact I've never forgotten) has been of no use at all to me in later life. I can't remember anything else about the subject, except that Miss Kavanagh, who taught it, always wore very low-necked knitted silk jumpers, and when she bent down we could see right down to her waist, which made us all giggle and nudge one another. Mrs Docherty taught maths, efficiently but boringly, but I knew I must work at this, as when I came to take my School Certficate exam in the upper fifth I should not achieve Matriculation standard without it. To obtain your School Certificate you had to gain a 'Pass' in at least five subjects, but Matriculation required you to gain at least a 'Credit' in all the five subjects you took, and must also include a 'Pass' in maths. (it was possible to acieve a 'Distinction' or 'Very Good' with really high marks). So, with a sigh, I applied myself to geometry, trigonometry (what on earth *are* logarithms – I still don't know), and simultaneous quadratic equations. There was nothing else to be done.

English, taught by Mrs Bark, a gentle lady in drab suits and men's pullovers, was an enthralling subject – under her tuition I even found grammar fascinating! We were given such interesting essays to write – poems, too – in which I revelled. Looking through some of my old Leamington College exercise books I find that somehow

I managed to turn every subject into something to do with the RAF. What Mrs B thought when she was marking my essays, I can't imagine – they were all filled with descriptions of the sound of Merlin engines, Wellington bombers, crews baling out and being picked up, raids over Germany – she must have got rather tired of it! But she still gave me very good marks, so as she was a very sympathetic sort of person, I expect she understood. Here's an example, written on the 9th November, 1942, which seems rather strange in the light of events earlier that year, of which more later. Whether we were given the title of the essay, or asked to write on the war in general, or maybe given the Churchill quotation to elaborate on, I don't remember. In any case, whatever was set, I'd have managed somehow to turn it into my favourite subject!

THE ROYAL AIR FORCE

"Never in the field of human conflict was so much owed by so many to so few." These immortal words were spoken by Winston Churchill in his great and memorable speech of 1940, when he praised the splendid work of the Royal Air Force. Hitler in boastful confidence had sent over large numbers of the Luftwaffe bombers and screens of long-range fighters; alas for his plans – the men of our lesser-equipped air force met the enemy and drove them back, thereby establishing Britain's air supremacy which she will never lose. Spitfires, Hurricanes and Defiants were the fighters mainly used in the glorious Battle of Britain, but now, in 1942, although Lightnings, Havocs and Tomahawks are replacing them, the Supermarine Spitfire Vb – faster and better armed – still flies on.

During the early part of the war, Britain's sadly deficient air force was compelled to be on the defensive, and to intercept German raiders. Now, however, with American help, these brave men are hammering hard at the heart of Germany and Italy. Giant multi-engined bombers fly nightly to important targets, and what joy and pride is felt in the heart of every Britisher as he hears 'all of our aircraft have returned safely from the night's operations.'

Greater than the wonderful aircraft that the RAF are using are the spirits of the men that fly them; gaily they set off on operations which take them countless miles from their base, with no thought for the future – only a boyish thrill of 'being on ops'. What youthful pleasure the crews find when they return home, in talking light-heartedly of the night's work amid laughter and teasing.

Aircraft have developed rapidly through this war. We began the war with Blenheims, Wellesleys, Hampdens and Wellingtons; these have increased in power and bomb capacity and now Stirlings, Lancasters, Halifaxes and Liberators have taken their place, the last and greatest achievement having been the De Havilland Mosquito – a light reconnaissance bomber reputed to have a very high top speed.

Not forgetting the aircraft factories, ground staff, service crews and those who have sacrificed their lives, I propose a toast – The Royal Air Force !

That could have been a piece of propaganda specially produced for the RAF, not the painstakingly-written essay of a fourteen-year old schoolgirl in a battered exercise book. But that's how I felt at that time – along, I'm sure, with a whole lot of other folk. It only received eight marks out of ten, but also Mrs Bark had written 'Good' at the end, in her neat red-ink script. And there *were* a few crossings-out, smudges and corrections – I think I got carried away by my enthusiasm, and could not set my thoughts down fast enough. Even the title we were set another time – 'a Great Bridge by Day and Night' – where it might be thought that you could get away from the war for a page or two – didn't escape a mention of the RAF where I was concerned! As you will see:

A GREAT BRIDGE BY DAY AND NIGHT

Westminster Bridge, standing in the midst of our beloved capital, spans the Thames, linking Westminster with Lambeth. Every hour of the day London's busy traffic roars across it in a ceaseless stream; cars and buses, lorries and bicycles, and now – during the war – convoys of camouflaged army vehicles bound for unknown destinations. Thirty-feet Royal Air Force lorries rumble ponderously over its surface, carrying their burdens of smashed enemy aircraft, and how proud the man in the street feels as he sees a broken, tattered swastika on the feebly flapping fin of a German bomber. Westminster Bridge sees all this in silence however, and adds it to the variety of scenes it has witnessed in the past.

Perhaps in the quiet of a Sunday evening, war forgotten for the moment, the great bridge hears the vibrant notes of the not far distant Westminster Abbey. In the daytime, on all weekdays, the bridge is never quiet – all is bustle and noise. The chug of a barge on the Thames and shouts of men intermingle with the dull roar of traffic and the jangle and rattle of crates and boxes on passing lorries.

As late afternoon merges into dusk, and dusk into night, the scene changes. Dim lights appear where in peace time all was lit up brilliantly. They are reflected feebly in the black waters below, and the outline of the bridge is silhouetted faintly against the sky. The night wears on, till the magic of dawn takes the place of the gloom.

The red sun rises and paints the steel girders with a rosy glow, and gilds each ripple of the mighty river. The smoke of the busy factories has not yet tainted the fresh air. For the early morning mists still hang over the river. The beauty and majesty of London's dawn upon Westminster Bridge are best described in the words of the famous sonnet:

'The river glideth at its own sweet will,
Dear God! The very houses seem asleep,
And all that mighty heart is lying still'.

The RAF only gets a small mention that time, but I manage to squeeze it in. Another subject we were given for an essay was 'Speed'. How do you think I began mine?

SPEED

The reverberating low-pitched note of a Merlin engine shatters the customary stillness of the British countryside, and the slender, perfectly proportioned body of a Spitfire flashes across the sky at more than four hundred miles per hour . . . .

Poor Mrs Bark – how patient she must have been!

'Greek' dancing was on the curriculum in those days, though anything less Greek it would be hard to imagine. For this unlikely exercise we were required to wear short ,skimpy, pale blue tunics which were most unflattering to our various adolescent shapes and sizes. Watching the unrestrained bouncing bosoms of some of the more well-blessed girls, I was quite glad of my rather less developed physique. We bent and stretched in curious Attic postures – meant, I presume, to promote grace and poise, or something of that sort. I don't know if it did.

Singing lessons were a delight to me. After romping through the excellent National Song Book at the Benson School, the standard of vocal training at Coloma had dismayed me. Everything was sung in unison, and the songs we were given were childish and banal. One particularly obnoxious ditty was about losing a sixpence and asking St Anthony (patron saint of lost articles) to find it, whereupon it miraculously appeared. Another started, 'Oh, how I love to go up in a swing, up in the air so blue' – I'll say no more. Here at Leamington College we had something to get our teeth into – Elgar's lovely 'Songs from the Bavarian Highlands', madrigals, and a Cantata 'The Banner of St George' – also by Elgar. Two – and three-part harmony was both challenging and rewarding. I was always asked to sing the second soprano line because I could keep to my part. I made friends with Janet Cambray, a very attractive girl with glorious red hair, also a second sop, who sat by me to hear what I was singing! We have never lost touch.

We were taught by Lionel Wiggins, who was organist at the imposing All Saints parish church, and an excellent musician. He was a dapper little man, immaculately dressed in a pale grey suit, spotless white shirt and grey tie with pearl tie pin. His elegantly styled silver hair completed the picture. And he certainly knew how to teach choral singing and to inspire his pupils. The results he achieved were impressive, and at Christmas time we explored the delights of the Oxford Book of Carols – a volume which I consider has never been surpassed. I joined the school choir and at assembly we sat on benches at the front of the hall, singing descants to the hymns; sometimes I sang a solo part. The one I particularly remember singing at a carol concert was a wonderful soaring descant to an arrangement of 'Silent Night'. With Christmas over – albeit a fairly austerity one – we began to look forward to the spring.

THE WAR GOES ON

In April 1941 we heard that Paul had now transferred to Wellingtons and was engaged in bombing practice and night flying. We realised that before long he would be operational and we would be in for some worrying times. In fact, in May, as we learned later, he was navigator and bomb-aimer on raids on Boulogne, and in June, Düsseldorf, Hamburg and Emden. These were night-time sorties and must have been traumatic. I imagined the air crews assembling on the tarmac in the dusk, climbing aboard the bomb-laden aircraft, taking off at a given signal and flying off into the darkness, all those hundreds of miles to Germany. Over the target the planes would be picked up by searchlights and subjected to a relentless barrage of anti-aircraft fire. Some would not return.

We did not always know at the time where Paul was based, but it seems that operations to Germany were carried out from RAF Alconbury. He never said much – his letters were cheery as always, and told more about films he'd been to and records he'd heard than anything about his RAF duties. He could not speak of them, of course. It is hard to think of him in connection with bombing anyone – a more gentle and less aggressive person it would be hard to find, and I'm sure the same applied to many of his colleagues. All Paul was really interested in was his playing his beloved trumpet in the band. When I heard what he was now engaged in, it inspired me to write with great fervour this fairly awful poem – but remember my tender age.

AN RAF RAID ON BERLIN

It's dusk on the runways, the hangars are dim,
The bombers are loaded with bombs for Berlin,
The men are all ready, the engines athrob-
And they are impatient to be on the job.
It's time that they started – the moon is on high
The bombers rise up to the lonely dark sky
In widespread formation they drone on their way
They pass o'er the Channel, bathed in the moon's ray,
They're over the target – the German guns roar
The observer stands ready to raise the bomb door,
The signal is given – the first salvo falls
It hits the objective and flames light the walls
The hum of an enemy fighter is heard-
Guns flash from our bombers – it falls like a bird,
The bombs are all spent – the planes turn for home,
In less than an hour they'll be back at their 'drome.
They cross o'er the Channel and land at their ground
And all of our planes have returned safe and sound.

I suspect that account is as far removed from the truth as it's possible to imagine. But it was my hopeful idea of what a raid on enemy territory was like. There are many errors, I'm sure. I don't think there were any night fighters at that time, there's no mention of searchlights or flak, and I really can't imagine what the bombers' top speed must have been if they could get back from Germany in less than an hour! In retrospect I think I may have been subconsciously reassuring myself that there was little danger to our air crews as they pursued their bombing operations, and that Paul would be in no danger in what he was doing. 'And all of our planes have returned safe and sound' I state happily. If only!

Back on the home front, on June 1st we were confronted with clothes rationing, and issued with the appropriate coupons. This state of affairs was quite a blow to everyone – particularly to adolescent girls just becoming interested their appearance and fashion in general. There was never any question of buying a smart new outfit, for all clothing had to be bought for its durability and usefulness. We were allowed sixty-six coupons per year, and children, who obviously grew out of things fairly quickly, were given ten extra coupons. Shoes, I remember, were five coupons a pair (seven for men), a skirt, six, and a blouse, three. Small sized clothes for children were correspondingly less. Means of economising on clothes became essential – old jumpers were painstakingly unravelled, the wool made into skeins which were then steamed to get the crinkles out, wound into balls and knitted up again. I can recall a jumper knitted for me which was made from two old ones – it was mainly scarlet with grey collar and cuffs. I thought it was rather chic. It was soon quite the fashion to let in a contrasting band of material as a means of lengthening a dress when it had become too short, perhaps adding a collar of the same to match up. Socks and stockings were darned again and again, faded coats re-dyed, and the best parts of adults' worn clothing used to make childrens' garments. These drastic economies came in gradually, when peoples' stocks of clothing from pre-war years began to dwindle. Skirts became shorter and pleats and full-skirted dresses were banned, so that a minimum of material could be used for each garment. Towards the end of 1941 'utility' clothing came into the shops. All these garments were stamped with the logo 'CC41' and made to exacting economy standards. Turn-ups on men's trousers were forbidden and the restrictions on the use of materials became even more rigid. Shoes came under these new rules, too, and later even 'utility' furniture, very plain in design and bearing the CC41 logo became available, the idea being that young couples must be helped to set up home in spite of the war. Unadorned and unexciting as these commodities were, they were all of quite good quality and made to last.

Hats – as far as I know – did not require clothing coupons, but during the war, who wore a hat ayway? Scarves and turbans came into fashion, the latter probably influenced by the ones women wore for protection from machinery in the munitions factories. They could be quite fetching, casual or smart, silk or cotton, and could be matched with whatever else you were wearing. There was a knack in tying them too, so that they would not come apart in the wearing. 'Jacqmar' silk sqares, though expensive, were very sought after, and I received a bithday present of a real beauty, emblazoned with army, navy and airforce badges and inscribed 'Combined Operations'. I would swank down the Parade with this casually thrown over my shoulders, feeling a million dollars. I wore and wore it until the design was almost washed away. A new sort of shoe for women appeared in the shops, just then – the 'clog'. This innovative footwear had brightly-coloured leather uppers and a wooden sole. We never really took to them, but many girls did – and they did not require clothing coupons, which was a great point in their favour.

At school the summer term meant cotton dresses – a relief to us all. Leamington College uniform ones were made from a rather attractive blue and white floral print and my mother soon ran me up a couple of these in the regulation pattern. After a while, however, other designs started to appear as girls grew out of their current dresses and the original print became unobtainable, though everyone endeavoured to stick to blue and white. We were ordered to guard our panama hats with great care, as who knew when new ones would – if ever – become available? My Coloma one, with new hatband, was more or less identical to the others – well, a panama hat is a panama hat, when all's said and done. How we hated them, wearing them on the back of our heads or at forbidden rakish angles, and taking them off as soon as we were out of sight of school in case we encountered any boys from the College.

There was not much skipping done during break times now that we were growing up. We preferred to stand around the playground in small groups, talking about films we'd seen, clothes we were saving up coupons for, and which College boys we'd met, or admired from a distance. Occasionally there would be a close huddle as someone imparted some shattering news they'd heard – once, that one of the senior girls had *'done it'*. In those unenlightened days I suspect we had only the vaguest idea of what 'it' was, but we all were suitably shocked and intrigued. We regarded the girl in question with great curiosity, wondering if this amazing rumour were true.

Paul came home on leave in June and informed us that he had volunteered for service in the middle east. He was excited at the prospect of seeing a bit more of the world We received the news with mixed feelings – obviously he would not get home on leave for ages, which was terrible. But perhaps he would be safer there than engaged in those long dangerous night flights over Germany, dodging the searchlights and flak, and from which so many of our aircraft failed to return – we just didn't know. But we did know we'd miss him dreadfully, for although we didn't see him very often, at least we knew he was in Great Britain – and there was always the telephone. It was very hard to say goodbye. He departed on June 26th from Harwell to Gibraltar, Malta and finally Kabrit, in Egypt, where 108 Squadron was stationed, though we did not of course know these details then.

There were posters everywhere with the caption 'Careless talk costs Lives'. I particularly remember one depicting a glamorous woman in the centre of a group of men. She obviously had some vital information which she (glass in hand, and most likely 'under the influence') was imparting to her friends in confidence – or so she thought. Behind the group lurked a sinister character, (he could only be a 'spy') listening avidly to what she was saying.
The picture carried a strong message. There were 'Careless Talk' films, too. Cinema programmes usually consisted of the main feature film, a 'B' movie, a news reel (containing plenty of propaganda), maybe a cartoon, and often a short film illustrating the dangers of indiscreetly passing on any information that might

be useful to the enemy. We paid one and nine pence for this substantial entertainment, which on the face of it would seem to comprise a very long programme. But feature films in those days were much shorter than the mammoth epics with which we are presented nowadays; the 'B' film was quite brief, and the news reel and cartoon only a few minutes each. Propaganda films were also fairly short and to the point. I once saw one which made such lasting impression on me that it was ages before I went to the cinema – or should I say, the 'pictures' – again. It featured as usual someone chatting indiscreetly in a public place and being overheard by an enemy agent. The result of this was the sinking of a convoy ship. Men were shown struggling in the water, and trying to board lifeboats under impossible conditions. The last shot showed a sailor's hand clutching feebly on to the side of a boat, the hold gradually loosening, then the hand sliding slowly down and disappearing beneath the waves. The stark caption then appeared on the screen: 'Careless Talk Costs Lives'. I was deeply shocked.

At school we often designed posters in art class, usually for different events organised to raise morale and promote the war effort, such as 'Dig for Victory', which urged everyone to grow more vegetables and fruit. Of course, my favourite was 'Wings for Victory' week, for which I painted three large 20 inch x 30 inch posters, one depicting an airman in full flying kit with a formation of bombers in the background, and another in RAF uniform against a squadron of Wellingtons. The third showed Britannia standing on the English coast, shading her eyes as she watched a group of Spitfires swoop past. Heady stuff! I made sure that the aircraft were perfect in every detail, and the face of every airman I ever painted was painstakingly copied from Paul's photograph. I wanted him up there for everyone to see. I suppose I was reasonably talented in drawing and painting, for commercial art was one of the possibilities I considered as a career years later, when making that all-important choice.

An airmail letter card arrived from Paul, written in July. He had sent a couple of telegrams to let us know of his safe arrival. Apparently there were no flying duties that month, so he seemed to be having a very good time:

Sgts Mess
RAF
108 Squadron
Egypt

Dear Mum,

I hope you got the telegrams OK. I haven't written before as I didn't know whether or not we were staying here, but apparently we are, for several weeks anyway. We've been here since the end of last month. There's not much to do except bathe and go to the camp cinema – I've been to the pictures 18 times already. We've been to Suez a couple of times. I bought a new watch, which I shall probably break, so now I'm broke! I went in the sea with a watch on at Gibraltar, but luckily it wasn't mine – only an issue one.

We are hoping to get some leave soon – after payday, & shall either go to Cairo, or somewhere in Palestine, probably Palestine, as it's cheaper there.

It's ever so hot here, much hotter than it was at home before I left, & it's the same every day, never any clouds. We're lucky having somewhere to bathe, though – and it's like getting into a warm bath. We have a lot of fruit here – I usually have 3 oranges a day, & we have melons, grapes and figs often. Chocolate is dear out here – about a half crown for ½ pound block of Cadburys, & then it's all soft.

I wish I'd brought my silk shirts out, as we can wear "civvies" in the evening, but still I bought a couple of silk shirts for about 7 bob each – and you don't need coupons out here!

There are a lot of natives here, in those long white nightdress things! We have one comes in and makes the beds, cleans the shoes and brings tea in the afternoons – he keeps asking for "baksheesh" though.

Every night lots of mosquitos, beetles and bugs and other nasty things come crawling over you, still I suppose you get used to it.

I haven't seen Jack Wilkinson or his brother yet, but I hope to run across them sooner or later. I won't be able to send anything for Cynthia's birthday, as it would take 2 or 3 months to get there, but perhaps if you bought something you could take the money out of the allotment.

Have my kitbags full of junk turned up yet? It's a good job we had to leave them behind, as I have 2 more full up now!

Well I must finish now & go for a swim. I will write again in a few days time. When you write, send it by air mail, as it will get here much quicker & I don't think it will cost very much extra.

Cheerio & love to all, & many happy returns for Cynthia's birthday.

Paul

This air letter arrived on 8th August – two days before my birthday, and sure enough, on the morning of the 10th there was a present from Paul, secretly bought by my mother – a 'thrilling schoolgirl yarn' called 'The School Enemy' – it's still on my bookshelf. He hadn't been able to write in it of course, so, carefully inscribed on the flyleaf in my best juvenile handwriting is the caption: 'To Cynthia from Paul, August 1941'. It was just like him not to forget my birthday in spite of being so far away, and in the midst of so many new distractions.

1941 wore on; life was getting progressively harder – less in the shops, queues for many things. My dear mother, true to character, had 'adopted' a mongrel terrier bitch called 'Nell' – all we needed in such a time of austerity. The dog belonged to a very poor family, who never fed her and let her roam the streets, with the consequence that she had innumerable puppies of every possible variety. My mother went round to their dilapidated house and offered to buy Nell for two pounds, which was enthusiastically accepted. We grew very fond of her, and with proper food and care she became much more presentable. But how to feed her when there was not even enough meat for ourselves, and any leftovers were kept carefully to make into something else? Pets had to be fed somehow, so a terrible horsemeat shop opened in Regent Street which sold only meat for dogs and cats – disgusting great pieces of flesh daubed with green dye in case it got into the human food chain by mistake. We didn't question where the meat came from, resolutely avoiding asking ourselves that question – dogs must be fed and there was no other way. The smell was dreadful – goodness knows how long this revolting commodity had been in transit. Still – needs must, and Nell wolfed it down with obvious enjoyment. A special saucepan was kept well apart from the others for her meat, and I must admit I always tried to be out when it was cooking.

Nell only had one litter of puppies while she was with us. In spite of our efforts to keep her in, she escaped on one occasion for a heady couple of days of romance with her old boy friend 'Monty', who belonged to Bishops the bakers in Warwick Street. "I'm going to get rid of her!" threatened my angry mother, when Nell's condition became apparent, but of course she didn't, and when the five puppies arrived she loved every one of them. Puppies in a flat are not ideal, and they would race through the rooms with much enjoyment and a great deal of frenzied yapping, not to mention a few hastily mopped-up puddles. They were found good homes when they were old enough, and though we missed them, it was quite a relief to return to normal.

Letters and airgraphs continued to arrive from Paul, sometimes in a bunch, after a week or two with none at all. Airgraphs were the means of communication that we most often used; there were forms on which you wrote your message, and this was photographed, sent by air (don't ask me how) and reached Paul in a much-reduced size – only about 4 ¾ inches x 41/4 inches. I received one from him at the end of September – he always included me in the letters he sent to my mother, but getting one of my own was very special:

917067 Sgt Morey
Sgts Mess
108 Squadron RAF
c/o HQ ME

Dear Cynthia

Thank you very much for the airgraph. I have sent an airmail letter card to Mum, but I expect this will reach you first. I hope you can read it, as I'm not much good at writing neatly. I'm glad you had so much money for your birthday – how much did you manage to scrounge off Daddy? So you are having a lot of rain, are you? I haven't seen any yet. I have just got back from leave in Palestine, & have been to Jerusalem & Bethlehem, and hope to go to Cairo in a fortnight's time. I got your letter with the drawings that you sent to Harwell. I wonder what the censor thought! Well, that's all there's room for, so cheerio & lots of love

Paul

Reading these letters now, with their superficial accounts of leave, and sightseeing, cinema visits, swimming and other relatively trivial activities, I can read between the lines and realise how much information had to be omitted. Paul was fully operational all this time – his log book tells us that. It must have been difficult to compose an interesting letter when he had to leave out all the drama, and dwell only on trivialities. Life was not all enjoyment – far from it.

I had actually managed to get a new bicycle in November – these things were occasionally available, though that seems rather surprising in the light of other privations. I had wanted one for ages, and had pestered my poor father for goodness how long. In fact, I finally prepared a 'legal' document signed by him (under duress!) and witnessed by my mother and Olga, which made him promise to buy me a bicycle! It read as follows:

PROMISE

I HEREBY PROMISE TO BUY: <u>Cynthia R Morey</u>:
A BICYCLE
   A) as soon as a suitable one can be obtained
   B) before <u>*CHRISTMAS 1941*</u>
   C) Either NEW or SECOND HAND (when it must be in an
   excellent condition)
ALSO THAT I WILL NOT PUT ANY OBSTRUCTIONS IN
THE WAY, <u>OR</u> SAY I HAVE NO MONEY,
                    for I must remember:-
   1) although I pay more Income Tax, I have not got to provide food
or clothing for Paul
   Or Olga
   2) I have not so much rent to pay
   3) I have 5 (five) shillings & 8 (eight) pence LESS school fees to
pay
   (per term)
   4) I WILL BE ASSISTED IN THE PURCHASE OF
AFORESAID BICYCLE
       <u>*NOR WILL I BUY CYNTHIA A CHEAP, SHODDY*</u>
                    <u>*BICYCLE*</u>
                       <u>*OR*</u>
       <u>*ONE THAT SHE DOES NOT WANT.*</u>

                    ————

      Nor, being an honourable gentleman, will I:-
I) Try to slip out of executing my promise
Ii) Say that I cannot afford the cycle
Iii) Refuse to take such steps as:-
     A) Advertising in the paper
     B Inquiring in shops In order to secure a bicycle
ALSO, IF OUR ADVERTISEMENT SHOULD BE
ANSWERED, I PROMISE TO ACCOMPANY MY
DAUGHTER TO THE APPLICANT'S HOUSE, AND IF

SAID CYCLE SHOULD PROVE SATISFACTORY, TO BUY IT WITHOUT FUSS.

I HEREBY SIGN MY NAME, BEING AGREEABLE TO ALL THESE PROMISES:-

<u>H.G. Morey</u>

(signed)

1st Witness: <u>O.M. Morey (signed)</u>

2nd Witness: <u>J.M. Morey</u> (signed)

<u>DATE: 8th September 1941</u>

Well! This document, written on a long sheet of cartridge paper, creased and dog-eared, still exists. I can no longer remember why my poor father had less rent to pay (perhaps Olga, now in a good job, contributed) or school fees that were five shillings and eight pence less per term. And I suspect that my sister, now immersed in the civil service, helped me with the wording of the agreement. But I got my bicycle – presumably we had to wait for one to be available – and it was bought new at Halfords. There was one special person I had to tell – I wrote to Paul at once:

6th Nov, '41

Dear Paul,

I got your airgraph safely. Don't they look funny when they arrive? Are you still eating oranges and dates? We all saw 'Target for Tonight' and thought it very good, and we all thought of you when we saw the observer.

I've got a marvellous bicycle! It's a Raleigh Sports model and it was £7.12s.7d. I want a cyclometer now, and a dynamo lighting set. The bike's got those nice caliper brakes and one of those new sort of saddles, and it goes very fast.

Well, I am nearly at the bottom of the page, but I must just say that we wish you a very happy Xmas. We've sent you some small presents, so I hope they'll reach you O.K.

Lots of love from

Cynthia

We didn't relish the thought of another winter, with little or no heating, either at home or at school. Olga was continuing to unpick old jumpers like mad and knitting them up again, and we carefully worked out what warm clothes it was absolutely necessary to buy with the few coupons at our disposal. More and more queues were to be seen outside shops, and it was customary to rush to the head of the line of people and ask, "What are they selling?" Sometimes it was something as ordinary (but essential) as a comb, or soap, or some other commodity that was in short supply. At other times nobody knew what the queue was for, so you just joined on the end anyway. There was a tale that someone stood for hours in an enormously long queue outside Woolworths, to find when they reached the counter that it was packets of birdseed – wonderful if you had a budgie, but otherwise not particularly useful. All sorts of unexpected ingredients were beginning to find their way into wartime recipes, but I don't think birdseed was one of them.

Just opposite where we lived on the Parade, in a top flat, lived Mr and Mrs Summerton and their daughter June, who was about my age. We soon became friends and used to go around together a lot, and very often to the swimming baths. June didn't have a telephone – strange to imagine it now, but at that time very many people didn't. We'd always had one owing to my father's work in the Post Office – or the GPO as it was then called. So June and I tried to work out some form of communication, as it was tiresome for her to come down all those stairs just to find out what time we were going to meet – or for me to climb all the way up to her flat, for that matter. So we devised an ingenious way to get in touch: June screwed a cotton reel on to the windowsill of her bedroom, and we placed a long length of strong twine round it, making sure that it would run freely. I went down into the street and she let down the two ends, weighted, so that they would descend without blowing out of my reach. I caught hold of them, June came down to join me, and first making sure the coast was clear, (remember, there was little traffic in those days) we ran across the road with the two ends of the twine. I went up to our flat while June waited below, ran into my bedroom and let down a string, to which June fixed the twine. I pulled it up to our balcony and put the two lengths round a convenient piece of wrought ironwork, pulled gently so that the twine was taut, and tied a knot. We now had a circular highway which I checked by pulling on one side of the twine; it went round easily. I gave the 'thumbs up' to June, who ran back up to her flat, then I wrote a quick note which I pinned to one side of the twine. I pulled the other side and off went the note across the Parade, and up to June's windowsill. Communications had been established – right across the main street of Leamington – what price e-mail?

Our mothers viewed our communications highway with a certain amount of tolerant disapproval, saying they were sure someone would come up and knock on our door and tell us to dismantle it. But nobody did. Everybody was much too busy with more important things. And unless a piece of paper was actually in the process of going across, the line was really more or less invisible. Letters went backward and forward every day, and we were extremely pleased with our efforts.

June and I got up to all sorts of things, including arranging to meet boys in the park or in the Jephson Gardens. These lads were mostly from Leamington College for Boys – the male equivalent of our own school, housed in a beautiful old building in Binswood Avenue. We talked freely about our activities in front of our parents – but in a secret language, which drove them mad, as they couldn't understand a word of it! We tried 'backslang' but that's rather easy to interpret, so adopted 'Yang-Tang' (also known as 'Aigy-Paigy') which is really unintelligible to the uninitiated, especially when it's rattled off at high speed, as we were able to do with constant practice. Explaining 'Yang-Tang' is very difficult. In short, it consists of putting the syllable 'aig' between the initial letter and the remainder of each word; for instance, the simple sentence 'How are you?' would be rendered as 'H-aig-ow aig-are y-aig-ou?' You'll notice that when the word begins with a vowel, 'aig' comes at the beginning. Really experienced speakers of this peculiar language can put 'aig' between every syllable of multi-syllabic words! By dint of regular use June and I reached this standard of proficiency, ensuring that our private chats when others were present about the boys we currently fancied remained absolutely confidential. I'm not sure of the origin of 'Yang-Tang' but some say it was invented by British prisoners in the first world war to foil their German guards. It certainly worked for us.

In the summer, the River Leam was the focus of our activities. It's a tributary of the Avon, and particularly beautiful around Leamington. Some times June and I would hire a boat (finances permitting). It could be a punt, (propelled by paddles, not a pole, as the river was deep in places) a rowing boat, or if it was a particularly fine day and we turned up late so that nearly all the boats were out, it might be the dreaded dinghy. We hated this because you had to row so hard without making much progress. When we were really broke and could only scrape a little money together, we were allowed to take out a punt which leaked, at half-price. One of us had to bale while the other paddled, which wasn't very enjoyable as it was hard work, so we didn't do it very often. I can't imagine that this would be permitted these days! Once we tried a canoe, but there is definitely skill needed for this. We found we spent more time in the water than on it.

At other times, when the weather was hot, we got on our bicycles and cycled to Radford Semele, which was then a small village, a few miles upstream. We crossed a couple of fields to the banks of the river, where usually quite a crowd of us turned up with our swimming things and a picnic, and spent the whole day there, only going home when the sun began to set. It does seem strange now to think that we dived or jumped into the water there without a thought about safety. It was very deep in places and there were patches of weed, which could have been extremely dangerous. We are much more conscious of these things now, yet I never heard of anyone drowning or getting into trouble.

All these escapades were of course played out against the dark grey background of war, but they provided us with some much needed light relief.

At fourteen, you couldn't be serious all the time. Life wasn't all fun, though, nor was it always summer, and another cold, cheerless winter approached. A momentous event occurred on December 7th – the Japanese bombed Pearl Harbour, destroying American ships and causing terrible destruction and loss of life. We had been receiving welcome aid from America for some time, but they had so far steadfastly refused to become involved in the conflict. Now they had no option. The next day, December 8th the USA and Great Britain declared war on Japan. It seemed we were in for a very happy Christmas.

The 'festive' season approached – without an awful lot of cheer, I must say; a couple of telegrams of good wishes came from Paul, and I received another airgraph all to myself, which I treasured. Apparently they were going to have a piano in the mess, Paul told me. 'Now I shall be able to make a noise!' he wrote gleefully. And he certainly made the most of that piano, as we heard later.

But how to provide some seasonal fare in times of rationing? More unusual recipes were added to the wartime cookery book. For some time red tins of dried egg had been occasionably available, also blue tins of dried milk. So a Christmas cake was devised using these ingredients. A tiny extra quantity of dried fruit was allowed, and my mother had been saving up any available sultanas and raisins for weeks, so altogether she had collected a respectable amount. Finding enough fat was a problem, and we were advised that liquid paraffin would be a good substitute! I can't remember what that cake tasted like, but, topped with a strange off-white icing made from dried milk, some old pre-war almond essence and goodness knows what else, it made some sort of seasonal centrepiece to our meagre Christmas table, and in any case, I'm sure our palates were becoming increasingly less discriminating by then. Limited extras were occasionally allowed on our ration books at such times so that our morale didn't sink too low, but it was nevertheless a fairly lean time. An airgraph to Paul from my mother, written on Christmas Eve confirms this:

Dear Paul

As you see I am writing this on Xmas Eve, just to let you know I am thinking of you. I am afraid our presents were not very large, but it was so difficult to know what to send to you out there. However, I hope the parcels have arrived safely, and that your Xmas was a happy one. We have had lots of cards, but as to Xmas fare, it is unobtainable. I have been trying for weeks to get some beer, but have not been successful, so it will be a dry Xmas. Yes, Daddy manages to get chocolate from 'Mr What's-his-name' at Warwick, also cigarettes. I think my New Year's resolution will be to give up smoking altogether!! Cynthia is studying aircraft as hard as she can. She has several books and learns the particulars of each by heart. She knows a lot of the technical terms. Are there any WAAFs out there? If so, have you fallen for one? I saw that film 'Cottage for Sale' with Leslie Banks and Jean de Cassalis. It was good. I have sent you twenty-two books altogether, & hope they will reach you safely.

Cheerio, all the best from all, love from Mum

I don't know who 'Mr What's-his-name' was, but good for him!

THE WORST YEAR

1942 – the third year of the war – arrived, bitterly cold. Mittens at school were essential in order to keep your hands warm enough to hold a pen, but we plodded on. I developed a strange rash round my neck which the doctor, somewhat puzzled, diagnosed as the result of vitamin deficiency. I don't remember any extra vitamins being offered, only an obnoxious khaki-coloured ointment which smelt disgustingly of tar. Surprisingly, there didn't seem to be any more coughs and colds than there are today, in spite of the constant freezing weather and lack of heating, probably fewer. Hot school dinners, cooked by Mrs Proctor, a fat jolly lady in a white overall, were served to those who wanted them – it usually smelt as if some sort of stew was on the menu, plus cabbage, of course. I preferred to go home for mine. I knew what was in my mother's stew!

An ordinary letter arrived in February from Paul, enclosing photographs showing his crew posed in front of their Wellington, taken before the squadron changed to Consolidated Liberators, vast four-engined aircraft. We studied them minutely, drinking in every detail. "They all look very well and suntanned," said my mother. "Paul seems to be enjoying life out there." He writes:

Dear Mum,

I am sending a few photos which I hope you will like. I haven't written much this year, as I have had 17 days leave already, and have spent a week going to Sumatra & back.

On our way out to Palembang in Sumatra, (which the Japs have now) we stopped at Karachi, & Bangalore in India, & on the way back, at Madras and Karachi. We had lots to eat, but not much rest, & at our hotel in Madras we had an eight course dinner, paid for by the RAF!

It was very hot at Sumatra, & is mostly jungle there, with lots of trees growing out of water & there were those houses on stilts there, with people bathing from their front doors! Pineapples were very cheap (about 1d each) and also bananas.

There is no blackout in India, & it seemed funny going through the streets in Madras, with the street lamps full on and all the shops lit up. It was quite nice there, but I didn't see any 'Poona-ites'.

Karachi wasn't very good, but I bought a camera there, costing £4-4s – no wonder I never have any money!

I have been on two leaves already this year, both to Cairo, & went to the pictures about 20 times!

Well, that's all for the present, so cheerio & lots of love,
Paul

It seems that all Paul could talk about in his letters was going on leave, having wonderful food and going to the cinema. What he could not tell us was that all through the autumn of 1941 and the first two months of 1942 he was fully operational, as we later found out, with much danger from flak, and once, on a raid, the aircraft was hit, wounding Steve Challen, the rear gunner, in the throat. Luckily he recovered and was soon back on operations. Those leaves, with their brief spells of relaxation were richly deserved.

We began to look forward to the spring, and the prospect of some warmer weather. On March 15th I was confirmed at St Mark's Church, having attended confirmation classes for several weeks previously. June and I went to Holy Trinity in Beauchamp Avenue most Sundays and she was to be confirmed the following year. My mother had somehow found the material to make me a white dress and veil for this important day, as was customary in those times. All the first communicants had managed to dress traditionally – it was easy for the boys of course, looking scrubbed in their clean shirts, but some girls no doubt had to borrow dresses for the occasion. June borrowed mine the following year, I recall. It was an inspiring service, but subsequent events wiped the whole thing from my mind completely for some considerable time. Much later I was to look at the date in the small prayer book presented to me after the confirmation service and say, 'Oh, yes . . . . I remember now . . . . that was the day I was confirmed . . . .'

March 16th dawned like any other day; morning school passed without event, and I was almost home for lunch when I saw my father standing on the steps outside the main entrance to our flat. 'What's Dad doing home from work so early?' I wondered, and quickened my steps, waving a greeting. Then I saw his face. It was like stone. And then he told me. A telegram – the telegram that every family dreaded more than anything in the world – had come: Paul had been killed in an air crash.

I ran up the stairs to my mother and Olga, and I really don't know what happened next. It was like a ghastly dream, and I couldn't believe the terrible news. I do know that my dear mother, in a kind of trance, tears rolling down her face, put our lunch on the table, and I know without a doubt – ridiculously – that it was minced meat and boiled potatoes – quite a substantial wartime meal. Why ever should I remember an incongruous detail like that at a time of such turmoil and distress? I can see my mother now, standing there with a saucepan in her hand, not knowing what she was doing. She served the meal like an automaton, and of course nobody ate it. We were all in a state of suspended animation, unable even to express our grief to one another – unable to express anything at all. At the usual time I put on my coat and hat and left for school. I didn't know what else to do. I don't know if I even said goodbye to my parents or Olga – they probably wouldn't have noticed anyway. I walked to school in a daze and went into the form room blindly, unaware of anyone or anything and sat down at my desk. I didn't cry, I was too numb.

Just as the lesson began, I was called out of class. Obviously my father had telephoned – my mother wouldn't have been able to – and informed the head what had happened. I was immediately excused lessons, and sent to spend the afternoon quietly in the gym changing room – a small room with a couple of comfortable chairs. A girl with whom I was very friendly at the time was sent in to keep me company. Her name was Phyllis Hunt. Did we talk? I don't know. That is as much as I remember. Going home after school and what happened thereafter was a complete blank.

Details of the days that followed have mercifully faded from my memory. We heard that the fated Liberator AL577 with nineteen RAF crew members on board crashed in Ireland, somewhere in the Morne mountains. Paul had been coming home.

A letter from to my parents, received much later from one of the four survivors, Sergeant 'Pat' Pattinson, a great friend of Paul's, gave us some poignant details of the tragic accident. I quote:

5th June 1942

In your present bereavement I extend my deepest sympathy; your son Paul was indeed a very close pal of mine and besides being a first class navigator, was also one of the best fellows I have come in contact with in the service.

I first met Paul when serving with No 40 Bomber Squadron at Alconbury, (near Huntingdon) in June 1941. Shortly afterwards he volunteered to serve in the Middle East. I volunteered to go out there with the rest of my crew in October 1941 and was both surprised and glad to meet up with him again in Egypt. We served in the same Squadron (108 Bomber) for five months and had some grand times together, times I shall always remember, together with a few other members of the Squadron.

I am sending this photograph of Paul, myself and three other members of my crew taken beside the Pyramids on our last leave together which we spent in Cairo. I am on the camel on Paul's right (without hat).

We left Egypt on March 15*th* in a Liberator (giant American four engined bomber); there were nineteen of us together with full kit on board.

Our mission to England was a special one; we were not coming back to stay. The nineteen fellows consisted of the ship's crew of which your son was navigator and three specially selected crews, with one flight engineer.

We left Egypt at 5pm (Egyptian time) and had a wonderful trip across the Medierranean and France; all this time we were right on course. The first indication of trouble was shortly after we flew over the French coast, heading for England. We ran into the worst weather I have ever experienced in three years of flying. It was impossible to see our own wing tips. We all knew we should require a good deal of wireless assistance if we hoped to get down safely. Then the real trouble began – the Wireless Operator could not contact any station in England because of some fault in the wireless equipment. We knew we were over England and we lost height to two thousand feet in order to enable us to pin-point our exact position, but the weather was just as bad at two thousand feet.

It would have been unwise to go down any further because of barrage balloons or mountains so we climbed up again and cruised around hoping for the weather to clear, but it did not; instead it became even worse. By this time we had been in the air over fifteen hours and we were carrying fuel for just over fifteen and a half hours. We were preparing to bale out and chance it but before we could do so someone spotted lights on the ground at about five hundred feet. About this time two of our four engines ceased running and we were nable to climb very well. The captain then headed straight along the coast of Eire to try to land at an aerodrome in Northern Ireland. We had been flying for about half an hour after leaving the lights and all this time we were gradually losing height. There was a terrific crash and when I awoke I found myself lying about twenty yards from the machine, which by this time was practically burned out . . . .

I would like to add that Paul died at his post and I shall always

remember him as a hero.
Yours sincerely
T.E. Pattison

We were hardly able to read this graphic account of the Liberator's last flight, it was so harrowing, but we felt we had to know the circumstances of the crash Later we received some small gifts Paul had been bringing back for us – silk handkerchiefs embroidered with 'Mother' and 'Sister'. They were slightly burned and stained with oil, which caused us further distress. After the war, Paul's RAF log book was sent to us. It contained details of the air raids he made over Germany and information about operations in the Middle East. This too was burned at one corner. We looked at it in silence. We could not look at one another. Nobody spoke. Each one of us was imagining Paul's last moments in that doomed aircraft. It was too terrible to contemplate.

The bodies of the dead airmen from the crashed Liberator were in due course returned to this country and Paul's funeral was held at St John's church, Shirley. We all felt that his happiest days had been spent there, with his friends and the music he loved. Before long a small memorial stone was added to his grave to commemorate two of his friends who failed to return from operations abroad. Looking through some old papers and photographs I came across the copy of a letter that one of them had written to be given to his parents in the event of his being reported missing or killed. I believe the writer was Pilot Officer Eric Grove, and it was given to us by his mother.

My darling Mum & Dad,
When you read this you will already have received a telegram saying that I am missing. Do not be unduly worried; if however after 3 months I have not been listed as a prisoner of war do not agonise yourselves any further, but resign your dear selves to the fact that I am in the good company of Paul, Alex and John, where I shall be waiting

for you both to join me, which cannot be very long now – we'll be playing solo again in no time if it is allowed where we are going.

I would like enough money to be given to Mr Evelegh to buy a new flag for either the cubs, scouts or rovers of the 9ᵗʰ troop when the war is over.

Would it be possible for something of mine to be buried with Paul (with his mother's permission) together with a joint epitaph written by my beloved sister Kath – Does this seem fantastic – only we were such good pals.

My dearest love to everyone
  Your ever loving and devoted son
    Eric

P.S.
No fellow could have had a finer Mum & Dad than I-.
Thank you for a wonderful -if short – life-
  Be seein' yer !

Eric was killed over Germany in June 1943.

Pondering over the Liberator crash years later, and wanting to know more about it, I managed to contact Steve Challen, rear gunner on all Paul's operations in Wellingtons, both over Germany and in the middle east. The RAF Association helped me to get in touch with him, and he wrote me several interesting and informative letters which helped me picture the life they led there.

'Paul and I got along very well together. We shared a tent until we moved into the new accommodation block at Fayid. I have fond memories of Paul at the honky tonk piano in the sergeants' mess playing all the latest and more. I was on hand most times with a glass of some of the terrible liquid they called beer.

Paul was an expert navigator. There were no complaints from our captain Ken Vare, a new Zealander in the peace time RAF. I never heard on the intercom Ken question or correct any of Paul's work for Germany, Gibraltar, Malta, Egypt, or our ops over the Western Desert. Late November 108 was to receive Liberator 4 engine aircraft. When the first one was ready for ops the C/O R.J. Wells DFC decided to be the first to try the new a/c on ops to Tripoli. He gathered up a scratch crew and Paul and I volunteered. Then early 1942 F/L Vare and crew were selected to fly a load of spares for Blenheim aircraft in Singapore. They were at a standstill without them. We took off from Fayid. Ten hours later landed at Karachi; next morning to Bangalore, refuelled, on to the far east. Some way over the Indian Ocean we were diverted by wireless to Sumatra. No problem for Paul, who changed course and landed at Palembang. Overnight, took off for Madras, India, then on to Habbaniya, Iraq, and on to base Fayid. Paul was the busiest one in the crew and right every time, the reason our crew was selected for the trip to England. Not S/L Vare, as W/C Wells decided to captain the flight himself. The gunnery leader late the night before take-off sought me out, telling me he was going in my place . . . .'

Lucky Steve Challen . . . . Fate is a strange thing.

How do people pick themselves up and get on with their lives after such a tragedy? I speak for all the bereaved families of that time – we were only one of thousands. My mother bought black armbands for us to wear, as was customary, and we were among many others displaying this sad symbol of their personal loss, The numbers of bereaved increased daily, but to me there was no need for any outward sign, for my inner distress continued unabated and there seemed to be no relief from it. I would wake up in the morning, momentarily forgetting the terrible tragedy that had torn our lives apart, then reality would suddenly come flooding back. Spring didn't come for us that year. The seasons changed, but we were only aware of an interminable greyness which stretched hopelessly into the future. Sometimes it was too much to bear. Yet gradually, almost imperceptibly, we pulled ourselves together. School kept me going and took my mind off the ever present sadness for a while each day. Olga was busy at her office and with her fire-watching rota, my father at work in Birmingham. I don't know, in retrospect, how my mother spent those dreadful days – I just can't imagine. The hardest thing of all was that cheerful air letters from Paul continued to arrive for several months, and made difficult reading. I didn't know until much later that my mother still wrote to him daily – she knew perfectly well that he had died, but she had to express her feelings somehow, and had bought a large hard-backed exercise book in which she wrote down all her thoughts. I did not find this until quite recently, and was deeply moved by it.

In retrospect, after what had happened, I would have thought that any references to the RAF would have been too painful for me to introduce into my essays any more. But no – I seemed even more inclined to write about it. Perhaps it kept Paul alive for me – I don't know. In my English exercise book later in 1942 I find 'A Parachute Jump'. The first few lines are as follows:

'*A burst of fire from the guns of a Messerschmitt 109F almost carried away the tail of my Hurricane, and I knew in a flash that I must bale out immediately or plunge to my death in the steeply-diving machine. I jumped free from the aircraft which was now blazing fiercely and began to hurtle towards the earth in a sharp, erratic dive . . . .*'

And a couple of weeks later there is this poem:

BOMBER CREW

It's a dark, still night.
What's that?
A low, distant hum – it comes
Nearer.
Nearer.
Till it grows into a roar.
A Wellington.
If we could look inside, what should we see?
Six men intent on their tasks,
The Pilot,
Captain,
Tall, gay, debonair,

His sensitive fingers stray over the controls.
The great plane responds to his touch like a good horse under
the hand of an experienced rider.
His strong profile gleams eerily in the dim light.
Second Pilot.
More commonly referred to as 'Second Dicky', 'Stooge'.
He sits beside his captain,
Ready, eager, anxious to help, ambitious,
But bored.
For he is only Second Pilot.
Front Gunner.
Peering into the blackness, guns ready.
Alert.
Sandy-haired, blue-eyed – a Scotsman.
And proud of it!
Observer, Navigator, Bomb-aimer.
The man of all work, cool, calm, capable, responsible, reliable.
Dark Hair and hazel eyes
That twinkle.
Only a boy, young, good-looking.
Wireless Operator.
Twiddling knobs, pressing buttons, tangled in earphones.
The only link to the far-off base.
Ginger-haired, freckled, snub-nosed, ugly.
But attractive!
Rear Gunner.
Isolated, lonely, waiting for his turn.
Brown-haired and lanky, his long legs cramped in the small
turret.
Engrossed in a thriller till over the target.
Completely rapt in the doings of someone else.
This is the crew.
Silent at the moment, but there will be ragging and laughing in
The mess when they get home.

Strange, perhaps, for a teenage girl to be writing this sort of thing, especially in the light of our recent tragedy. How I could bear to do it, I don't know. But I suppose it was a way of keeping Paul alive for me – it's not hard to recognise him in that poem. Of course, it's rather sentimentalised and very likely completely inaccurate, but it was my own idea of the crew of a Wellington. Setting it down like that was probably the equivalent of my mother's writing to her son in that sad book. We all had our own ways of dealing with our grief.

PICKING UP THE PIECES

I gradually began to realise that singing was becoming very important to me. There were two reasons for this; the classes at Leamington College were extremely good, with interesting and challenging part songs, I was in the school choir, and also there was the fact that my mother had been an excellent soprano and had passed on her love of singing to me. It was announced that there was to be a school concert at the Town Hall, and that it would include a section of Coleridge Taylor's 'Hiawatha's Wedding Feast'. As there would be no male singers, Mr Wiggins needed one of the girls to sing the famous tenor aria 'Onaway, Awake, Beloved' and announced that anyone who was interested could go and see him in the staff room at the break. Could *I* do this, I wondered, and decided yes, I'd have a go. I duly presented myself to Mr W and must admit that he did not seem at all surprised to see me. "I'd like to sing Hiawatha's solo, please, Mr Wiggins," I said. "Do you think you can do it?" he asked. "Oh, yes," I replied – confidently on the outside, but there were a few butterflies within. He arranged to go through the song with me later to see if I could cope with it. This he did, and lo and behold – the part was mine. My mother was delighted, and of course was the ideal coach, which gave us both temporary relief from our distress. In no time I had learned the song by heart, and – more importantly – had learned *how* to sing it, with all the feeling and interpretaion it needed. What an exciting night that was. I can't remember much about anything else, what comprised the rest of the programme, or even what we all wore, which was almost certainly our school uniform; anything else by that time being out of the question. I still remember the thrill of standing up in front of a large audience (this has never faded) and performing. Of course I was nervous – who wouldn't be? But as soon as I began to sing, all nerves vanished, and I loved every minute of it. At the end of the concert I received a bouquet – my very first! It was probably quite a modest one, given the austere times, but I thought it the most beautiful thing I had ever seen. A memorable evening indeed, and a respite from the pervasive sadness that inevitably remained with us for many years.

At Christmas it was decided that the seniors should put on one of the Coventry Mystery Plays. This contained scenes depicting the Annunciation and the Nativity, and my friend Janet was cast as the Angel Gabriel. Most of the rest of us, apart from the Holy Family, were various citizens of Coventry – I believe I had a solo to sing – probably something in the lovely Coventry Carol. It was easy enough for us to find long skirts and shawls – we were only poor folk, and could easily look shabby, (we were used to that by then) but how would the Angel be dressed in such austerity times? Some wartime angels had been known to devise costumes from old white sheets, but that wouldn't do at all for us – we wanted *our* angel to look spectacular. I told my mother about it and she looked thoughtful. "Wait a minute," she said, "let me have a look in that old trunk – it's stacked away in the hall." There were no cupboards in that flat, so things were apt to get 'stacked' in various places. We unfastened the trunk – it was full of ancient bits and pieces which we thought might come in useful some time, but never had. My mother delved to the bottom and drew out something amazing. "How would this do?" she asked. It was a shining silver lamé dress – creased, of course, but there was no denying its possibilities. And, sure enough, when the day of the performance arrived, there was Janet, clad head to foot in silver, which set off her lovely auburn hair to perfection, looking sensational as the Angel Gabriel. "Good old Auntie Ellie!" we thought. That flamboyant dress could only have come from *her.*

That year we were all faced with the introduction of the 'national loaf'. This was said to be made from wholemeal flour and to incorporate more grain content than that of white bread, thus less waste. It bore no resemblance at all to the wholemeal loaf we know today, being grey, rather than light brown, rather dry in texture, and with a crust which tended to become hard. Imagine a slice of that, spread thinly with block margarine – not the most appetising prospect. Mind you, there might be jam as well – there were a few ambiguous flavours of this about, masquerading under the description of 'mixed fruit'. It was mainly based on marrow, I suspect, and tasted like it. Some fairly flavourless quince jam imported from Australia was occasionally available but there was nothing to choose between these varieties. And that's if you had enough points left from essential groceries to buy any jam at all. Generally speaking, we were not enthusiastic about the national loaf – in fact I heard it described as 'Hitler's Secret Weapon', though I wouldn't go quite that far.

There were many Czech and Polish soldiers stationed around Leamington at this time and we would see them often in the town. They were courteous and friendly, made a very good impression, and were welcomed into people's homes. A Czech folk dancing club was founded, called 'Sokol' (I'm not sure what that meant – help me, any Czech readers!) where we learned the national dances of Czechoslovakia – it was an all-girl affair, and we threw ourselves into it with great energy, gyrating, clapping and stamping like mad, in what we imagined was true eastern European style. We even contrived some 'national' costumes, the like of which I'm quite sure had never been seen in Czechoslovakia, or anywhere else, for that matter. My skirt was made from an old orange curtain, with bands of braid stitched round the hem. With this I wore a white blouse with puffed sleeves and a waistcoat of black velvet, (I don't know where this came from, but it certainly wasn't new) and laced up down the front. Our head-dresses were a cluster of artificial flowers with ribbon streamers. Luckily, ribbon was not on coupons

– if you could get it, that is. We felt terribly authentic as we threw ourselves into the dance with abandon.

June's mother, still being of an age to be drafted into war work, was recruited as a shop assistant in Woodward's, a department store on the corner of Regent Street and the Parade. Many older women took up these jobs, thus releasing younger ones to join the services or go into munitions factories. This could occasionally be useful, as she worked on the haberdashery counter, so we were all right for a few yards of elastic from time to time. No doubt that's where I obtained the ribbons for my 'Sokol' head-dress. I'm afraid that the secretive selling of 'under the counter' goods was a fairly frequent occurrence. If you were on good terms with any shop assistant, you would be sure to know when a delivery of certain rare commodities was expected, and maybe something would even be put by for you.

Whereas the Czechs and Poles had been welcomed, it was another matter when the Americans, or 'Yanks' arrived in town. In no time at all the saying 'over-paid, over-sexed and over here' became common parlance, and, in spite of the many nice men among them, it wasn't long before American soldiers in general acquired a predatory reputation. Any girl seen hanging on the arm of a 'Yank' was frowned upon by the respectable matrons of Leamington. "She'll come to no good," they muttered darkly to one another, and to tell you the truth, they were not always wong. Enamoured girls would hang out at 'the Donut Dugout' – a very American café in the lower part of the town. There were a number of hurried weddings, but as some of the soldiers were already married, quite a few girls who had been 'caught out' had to bear their disgrace (and that is how out-of-wedlock births were viewed in those days) as best they could. There was a branch of Richard Shops on the Parade, and in the window one day was a dress with 'Got any gum, chum?' emblazoned across the bodice. "Oh, can I have that?" I begged my mother, "I've got enough coupons." "Certainly not!" she replied in horror, "It's disgusting!" I was very disappointed.

In spite of the seemingly endless depression and deprivations of the war, schoolwork proceeded apace, as ineed it must, for the prospect of the School Certificate exam loomed ever closer. My essays continued to portray the war, and in my exercise book, dated September 20th 1943, I find the following (and highly improbable) story:

THE ROOM UPSTAIRS

Miss Amelia Jones was a typical spinster. She led an ordered, uneventful life in a respectable flat in Marina Court, an unimposing block of flats just off the main road, modestly screened by two rows of stately elms. She rose at seven and retired at nine-thirty; she maintained a benevolent attitude to the world in general and busied herself in the welfare of two sleek cats, and fed the birds which assembled on her window sill each morning with admirable regularity.

One morning, Miss Amelia opened the window to feed her birds, and in brushing away some of yesterday's crumbs, caught her finger in a piece of wire which appeared to run along under her window sill. She craned her neck and followed the offending wire with her eye and found that it led to the room upstairs.

This annoyed Miss Amelia. The people upstairs were nuisance enough with their subdued talking late into the night and the continual thuds and taps which came from their flat. To an observant person the wire, together with the happenings upstairs, might have caused suspicion, but to Miss Amelia it was a hindrance to birds, and as she could be very determined on rare occasions, she fetched a pair of scissors and cut it through, separating the ends of the wire and pushing them away from her window. Her anger having abated, she proceeded to minister to her feathered friends as usual.

The next day, Miss Amelia Jones started from her easy chair at the sound of a forceful knock on the door. She hurried to answer its summons and stared in astonishment at the two police officials who stood outside.

"May we have a word with you, madam?" inquired the taller man.

She ushered them into her tiny sitting room, begged them to be seated, then awaited the tidings expectantly.

The shorter one of the two cleared his throat. "Early this morning, two German agents were arrested from the room above you, Madam" Miss Amelia clutched at the arms of her chair and gasped at the Inspector.

"They received a vital piece of information last night and had been trying to transmit it for two hours when we broke in on them. Something which we have not yet determined fortunately stopped them, and we have come to investigate from your window, if you please, Madam."

Miss Amelia fluttered with excitement. "Of course, Inspector. This is my window." The two men walked over to the small window and threw it open. Suddenly one gave a long whistle of astonishment, at the same time holding up two cut ends of wire. "This is the answer to our question," he grinned, "now this has been deliberately cut." "Oh yes!" gushed Miss Amelia. "It did so get in my way when I fed the birds, so I cut it. The people upstairs were so objectionable!"

The two men gazed at each other incredulously. "Well Madam," said the shorter one, "You have certainly done your country a great service. Had that piece of news been sent, one of our convoys would have been in great danger, and several ships would probably have been lost. No doubt you will be publicly thanked later."

Miss Amelia heard no more. In a daze she showed the officers out and resumed her seat in the easy chair. A blissful smile spread over her face. She had helped in the war – she had alsost certainly saved many lives. She sighed happily and stroked her cat. "And those objectionable people in the room upstairs have gone at last," she murmured with great satisfaction.

I was awarded nine out of ten for that improbable epic, and a footnote was added in red ink which read 'Good Characterisation'. Praise indeed. And for once, no mention of the RAF, though there was still more to come on that subject. I wonder now how I could continue to write about aircraft and personnel after the tragedy we had suffered. Yet I did, turning every subject, however far removed from matters aeronautical, into an essay which dealt specifically, and in detail, with the RAF. How could I bear to do this? I don't know. I can only think that it helped to keep Paul alive for me. Maybe I deluded myself into thinking that somehow he might be coming home when the war ended, though of course I knew perfectly well that he would not. The disturbed psychology of an adolescent faced with such turbulent events is hard to fathom. On September 27th we were given the topic of 'Dawn' for our weekly essay. No need to guess how I dealt with it.

The dark clouds of night which had obscured the harvest moon had begun to drift away, and in the east the sky was light and streaked with pale pink. As the rosy light began to steal over England, to the Englishmen in three entirely different situations dawn was once more bringing the prospect of a new day and new hope.

Far out to sea a large, round cumbersome object was floating on the waves. It was a rubber dinghy, and seated inside were six young airmen in various attitudes of repose. The rear gunner, a long, lanky boy with tousled hair, turned over on to his back and snored loudly. (here Mrs Bark put a note in the margin: 'In a *dinghy?*' I think she has a point) *The second pilot, who was sitting next to him, opened his eyes and sat up, glancing at the sleeping gunner. Putting his hand over the side, he scooped up some water and poured it into the sleeping gunner's mouth, at which he choked and sat up with a start. John, the navigator, who was sitting at the other side of the dinghy, mumbled sleepily, "Whass'up? Time to get up?" and sat up, rubbing his eyes. "Wake up, you fellows – it's morning. Want a cup of tea?" One by one the crew of the shot-down Wellington awoke to find that dawn had come. Suddenly, 'Tiny' the rear-gunner, who incidentally was six foot two, cried, "Quiet a minute, boys, listen!" A hush. A hum, almost imperceptible, elusive, reached the ears of those men – nearer, nearer. "Quick, Tiny – give me your lighter," ordered the captain, who then* signalled desperately. The huge figure of a patrolling Sunderland, shining in the light of dawn, circled three times in the air and glided down on to the water. Within three minutes the crew were on their way home.

At the same time a man stood in a despondent attitude on the deck of a lurching cross-channel steamer. It was the same hour, but five years previous to the crash of the Wellington and the rescue of the six men. The man, who stood grasping the rail and gazing into the angry sea was on his way to Dover, having boarded ship at Calais the night before. He lifted his eyes to the sky in the east and studied the pink and grey clouds disinterestedly, thanking God that it was dawn at last, and that the horrors of the rough crossing were nearly over. Soon he would be back on familiar soil after a year in a foreign country, and then he would be home with his wife and baby son and need not go away again, as the business to which he had been attending was completed. The sea appeared to be quieter now, and the motion of the ship, if not pleasant, was at least bearable. He strained his eyes into the half light and saw the welcoming white cliffs of Dover in the greyness of an autumn dawn.

Far away a convict stood at the barred window of his cell, staring unseeingly across the prison quadrangle at the gaunt grey walls opposite. This was the last night in his cell, he remembered without interest, for by noon he would be a free man. "Two years in prison," he recollected. "Two years of hard work, and I'm no better for it. What have I to look forward to?" From his narrow window he could just see some trees, behind which the sky was growing red with the dawn. Suddenly his depression dropped from him like a cloak. He would make good – he would get a job and work hard at it. The light of dawn stole over the prison. This was his last morning here, after all. He was practically a free man. So instead of gaining his freedom with a sullen hopeless attitude, he left the prison with a face full of hope and a brain full of bright prospects for the future. Five years later he was in a regular job, steadily gaining prestige and with a wife and family of his own.

So dawn, with its usual reputation for new hope, had come to three different places, bringing rescue to the airmen, a happy home-coming to the traveller, and the prospects of a new life to the convict. So, when this war is over, when bombs and tanks are a thing of the past, and when the lights of London shine brighter than ever before, a new world will dawn upon the ruins of the present one, and peace will reign unopposed.

When I read this after so many years, I cringe at the sentimental outpourings – most certainly if I'd been a bit older, I might have pursued a highly successful career writing propaganda. Then I have to remind myself that I was after all only fifteen, things were different then, and there was a lot of morale-boosting patriotism around. We were a war-weary society by 1943, deprived of so many things we had always taken for granted. Young people like myself, almost at school leaving age, had no idea what sort of career they might be able to pursue, for the future was so uncertain. Yet at no time was there ever any doubt that victory would be ours eventually – but when?

THE LONG HAUL

Leamington College for Girls
English Homework November 15th 1943

RECIPE FOR A SPY STORY
  Take an East End night club of doubtful reputation; add a ravishing
blonde well rolled in mystery and a susceptible young government
official. Season with the theft of some important documents and simmer
on a low gas until the whole situation becomes hot, then flavour with
a few violent deaths. Add a sprinkling of distracted policemen and stir
well till the mystery is solved. Throw in a hectic love affair and serve
hot with a happy ending.

This short essay is teamed incongruously with a homily on the
characteristics of the English:

Before the war we lived in a kind of perpetual night by the fireside.
Now and then we would raise ourselves condescendingly from our
armchair of complacently to draw the curtains of our island and look
out on the ever-changing panorama of the world, pulling the curtain
hastily at the sight of anything which might disturb the tranquillity of
our existence. Such was England's attitude to life before the war, but
if procrastination and self interest are characteristic of Englishmen
so then is adaptability, for our country in time of war plans for the
future; gone is the complacency of the pre-war days; it is replaced by
courage, determination and alertness.

Elevenses at Burgis & Colbourne, Leamington, 1943

I'm back to writing propaganda again – and rather priggish stuff, at that. And what about Wales, Scotland and Northern Ireland? Today, if such a piece were written at all, for 'England' you would have to write 'Britain', or. more boringly, 'UK'. However, in 1943 the content was received without comment, for the two short essays were awarded nine plus marks out of ten, and a star.

Although we didn't know it at the time, in 1943 we were more than halfway through the war, and in retrospect I believe that our morale was at its lowest point. In families like ours – and there were so many – who had lost a dear relative, spirits were low. Rationing was biting hard, and those people living in flats longed for a garden to be able to grow fruit and vegetables in order to supplement the limited selection available in the shops.

But life had its lighter moments. There was a wonderful department store on the Parade called Burgis and Colbourne. It occupied premises which extended right through to Bedford

Street, a small street that ran parallel to the Parade, and it was also known as 'The Bedford Stores'. The shop was rather old-fashioned, even for those days, but much esteemed by the residents of Leamington. I constantly visited the art department, trying to obtain art materials, which were in fairly short supply. Drawing and painting were becoming a favourite pastime. I became on good terms with the assistant, Mrs Austin, another lady who had been drafted into 'war work', and she would try to keep for me the things I needed if and when they were available. Jars of poster paint, brushes, sketch books and large sheets of cartridge paper – though deliveries were few and far between – did filter through from time to time. But the best place in the store was the restaurant on the first floor, where everyone would congregate for morning coffee. I often used to go with my mother on Saturdays or during school holidays, and I do believe that the camaraderie and warmth of the friends we met in that café helped her through that difficult time. She had begun to smile again – not often, for one with such a sense of humour, but now and then. We would enter the restaurant and immediately someone would wave, and we'd go and join them at their table. Then others would come, and pull up chairs until there were about a dozen round the table, all chatting and discussing the latest shortages or scandals. There was always someone with a story to tell. "You know that young girl who works at Boots? On cosmetics – the one with the blonde hair?" We nodded, in eager expectation. The voice would go down to a whisper, and all would lean forward. "Well, she's in *trouble* – and it's one of those Yanks." There would be a general gasp, and an exchange of exasperated looks. "But she's only about seventeen! I suppose there'll be a quick wedding?" someone would say. (such mishaps had to be legalised in those days). "Ah," said the bearer of the scandalous news, "I don't think so." Everyone waited with bated breath for the final revelation. There would be a (pregnant) pause, timed to perfection. Then would come the shocking finish to the sorry tale, delivered with a dramatic flourish: "There *can't* be a wedding. He's married already." There would follow a general shaking of heads and an exchange of disapproving looks.

Such a tale would necessitate another round of coffee. I can't remember what standard of coffee we were drinking by that stage of the war, but I suspect it was a pretty ersatz blend. Never mind – it was the company and the escape for an hour or so from the tedium of everyday wartime life that counted. We were served by a waitress called Gladys, and she did become rather exasperated when the crowd at our table became so large that it was difficult to manoeuvre her way among the chairs with a laden tray. However, we always collected a decent tip for her at the end of the session. I'm not sure that my mother was entirely comfortable about some of the scandals reaching my fifteen-year-old ears, but then, we'd all had to become broad-minded during those war years. And she probably thought that the dilemmas these poor girls faced would be a warning to me not to go down that road.

Just occasionally we would treat ourselves to coffee, or perhaps afternoon tea at the Pump Room, a beautiful regency building at the bottom of the Parade close to the river, where it was possible to try a sample of spa water. I thought this tasted really disgusting, though it was supposed to contain all kinds of health-giving minerals. In the tea room, music was provided by Van der Venn and his Trio, and we were regaled with selections from 'The Desert Song' or 'The Quaker Girl' or some gems from Gilbert and Sullivan. The maestro, who looked extremely English despite his name, sported a dashing black velvet jacket and a bow tie, and wore his abundant white hair fairly long. He was quite a personality, and gave the impression that playing in a café was really rather beneath him. On special occasions he would favour us with a virtuoso rendering of Massenet's 'Méditation from Thaïs'. His flamboyant technique caused surreptitious giggles from our table, but we joined in the polite applause with enthusiasm.

In January 1943 severe air raids on London were resumed. We felt very glad to be away from Croydon, and intensely sorry for the bombed-out Londoners and all the danger and destruction they were suffering. We knew what it was like to spend hours in the air raid shelter and to dread the constant sound of the siren. Leamington had a number of air raid warnings and even a scattering of bombs when the Luftwaffe attacked Birmingham, twenty-one miles away, but we were very lucky compared with others in more vulnerable areas. The coming of spring at last brought the usual lifting of spirits; it was so much easier to put up with the general deprivation and the depressing war news when the sun was shining. Suddenly there was a news item which filled us all with pride: a major air offensive had been launched – nineteen Lancasters of the specially-formed 617 Squadron had bombed the Moene and Eder dams in the Ruhr, using an amazing new 'bouncing bomb' designed by Barnes Wallis. These four-engined planes had replaced many of the old twin-engined variety, and were extremely efficient. It is difficult, with what we know now, thanks to comprehensive books and of course the famous film 'The Dambusters', to recall exactly how much we were told about the raid at the time. I am pretty sure that we were not informed of the loss of eight of the nineteen aircraft and fifty-three men. And we know that the damage inflicted was exaggerated, though there is no doubt that major flooding and disruption was caused. What inspired the British public and raised morale at such a crucial time was the incredible bravery of those air crews, led by Guy Gibson, braving intensive flak to fly in at an incredibly low level. We felt so re-invigorated. The whole country was once again confident of eventual victory. As for me – my rather undeveloped bosom swelled with pride. The RAF had done it again.

A GLEAM OF HOPE

For a couple of years running, Janet and I delivered Christmas mail, which entailed getting up very early for a week or so and working from about eight o'clock till lunch time, including on Christmas day itself. People still sent one another cards and presents, and obviously, with so many postmen now in the services and others engaged in war work, there were serious staffing problems, so older school pupils were invited to volunteer to give a hand. It was quite a hard job, starting work on a cold morning before it was light, but we were reasonably well paid, and extra cash was always useful. The bags of mail were fairly heavy, but Janet and I had an advantage over the other volunteers – our postal round was the nearest to the Post Office. This came about through my father, who, working in Birmingham and knowing the Postmaster of the Leamington office, had put in a word for us! Some of the girls were taken to their more far-flung rounds in post office vans, but Janet and I would stumble out of the GPO, wrapped up in our thick coats and scarves, shouldering our bulky mail bags, and turn immediately left into up Leam Terrace. Then away we'd go, she on one side of the road and I on the other, delivering the Christmas mail in the immediate vicinity. It was still hard work though, but we got the feeling that we were 'doing our bit' for the war effort at least. When we had small packets or oversized letters and calendars to deliver, we'd have to knock the door and hand them in. The festive spirit, temporarily replacing wartime dreariness, inspired people to dispense mince pies generously, especially on Christmas Eve, and one day I ate a dozen! Extra dried fruit had been allowed at this season, and I presume that a limited supply of mincemeat was available on 'points'. I should have put on several pounds, but I probably worked it off easily; many of the lovely old Georgian houses had flights of steps up to the front doors, and those, combined with all the walking kept us in trim.

Another move awaited my father as the war moved into its fifth year, this time to west London. He was to be promoted to the position of Head Postmaster in Hounslow, and soon after peace was declared, would establish the first post office at the new Heathrow Airport. In his chosen profession he had risen from office boy to quite an exalted job, which was really very commendable. So off to London he went at the beginning of 1944, to be greeted soon after his arrival by the first of the V1s, or 'doodlebugs' as they became known. It was decided that we should remain where we were. There was absolutely no need for us to return to such a danger zone, especially as my education was reaching a crucial stage, and we were more or less comfortably settled. We still hated the dilapidated and inconvenient flat and were constantly looking out for better accommodation, but there was absolutely nothing available. So we made do, like so many other people during those dark days.

The V1 was a pilotless aircraft carrying a ton of high explosives. Its engine made a rasping sound as it approached, and would suddenly, and without warning, cut out. That was the moment when terror struck, for the 'flying bomb' would plunge to earth in ten seconds and explode, killing many civilians and destroying buildings. My father described vividly how, when you heard one coming, you would hope and pray that the engine wouldn't stop, but go on to explode somewhere else. Not a kind sentiment towards the eventual victims, but it was every man for himself in such frightening times. Later we learned that the Germans had launched between 8,000 and 9,000 of these missiles on London and the south-east, but that nearly fifty per cent had been intercepted and destroyed before they could fulfill their deadly mission. A few Spitfires became adept at turning them over with their wing tips so that the 'doodlebugs' would plunge harmlessly into the channel or into a field.

In June, 1944, an even greater menace threatened London – the V2. This was a rocket, launched from bases in Norway, which travelled at over 2,000 miles per hour, at a great height, and approached silently. Whereas the V1 attacked indiscriminately, the V2 could be targeted. Nobody knew when it was coming – suddenly there would be a gigantic explosion as one of these evil things smashed down with no warning at all, and devastated everything in its vicinity. Londoners were in a constant state of apprehension and fear, not knowing when or where the next V2 would come crashing down. Hitler was obviously determined to destroy London and its inhabitants, and one of these diabolical weapons fell on a block of flats in Stepney, killing a hundred and thirty-three people. That appalling instrument of death and destruction did more psychological damage to morale than anything which had preceded it. There were 115,000 casualties. The RAF, with their new Mosquito aircraft destroyed many of the V2 launch pads, but enough rockets got through to cause havoc. It was a dreadful and demoralising time for Londoners, who had already suffered so much from the blitz. We mourned for them and hoped my father would be safe.

My last year at school arrived. Miss Ford, our biology teacher, decreed that all girls in the Upper Fifth should undertake an ecological project. "There will be a prize for the best entry," she said. We were required to choose a habitat in the local area – it could be a hedge, a field, a wood or a pond – anywhere that contained a varied collection of wildlife, and to monitor the creatures that inhabited it, recording in notebooks details of what we found, and the seasonal changes that occurred. We were to work in pairs, so Janet and I picked a pond in a field in Lillington, only a mile or two from the town centre, and easily accessible on our bicycles. We started out with great enthusiasm, making notes of what we saw, with accompanying drawings. Quite soon the enthusiasm waned, visits became less frequent – especially in bad weather, then finally petered out altogether. Time elapsed, then one day Miss Ford announced at the end of a biology lesson: "Don't forget, girls, your habitat notebooks must be given in next week without fail." Janet and I looked at each other in consternation. We thought of our books and the sparse details they contained. Why hadn't we gone to look at our pond more often? What on earth could we do? I set to work at once, consulting biology textbooks, anthologies of wild flowers, volumes on wildlife. I wrote, sketched, and stuck in appropriate bits and pieces every night after I'd finished my homework. "You *must* go to bed now," said my mother as the clock struck nine . . .ten . . ten-thirty . . . "Just another five minutes," I'd beg, "Let me just finish this diagram of the life cycle of the common frog . ." She'd agree, reluctantly. In a week's time I'd finished my fictitious account of 'A year at Lillington pond', lent it to Janet so that she could copy a few bits and pieces into her book, and handed it in. I won first prize. What a dishonest thing to do, you will say, and you'd be right. But the prize was an unbelievably boring book on fish, which I opened only once, and discarded for ever. All my frenzied work for *that?* It served me right.

The buildings in Leamington were beginning to show the effects of the war, of years without maintenance of any kind, and only absolutely essential repairs carried out. The fine regency houses looked sad and run-down, with crumbling stucco and peeling paint. Windows here and there were boarded up, railings had been taken for their metal content, and the fine Parade looked drab and neglected, its once-luxurious shop windows half empty. Part of the beautiful Jephson Gardens had been dug up, and vegetables planted, though I have heard it said that the project was rather half-hearted – more of a gesture than a real contribution to shortages. All the public gardens looked drab and tired – as do doubt we ourselves did.

Yet from the time of the Dambusters' raid in 1943 a subtle change had come over the country. We sensed that we were reaching a turning point. We knew the end of the war was still far off, but somehow we felt for the first time that we were actually going to get there. The Allies were doing well in Africa, and invaded Italy. Mussolini had been deposed, and the new Italian Prime Minister had signed an armistice with the Allies. Things *had* to be looking up. And in 1944, not long after my father went to London, rumours that the launching of the Second Front was imminent were rife. Crudely chalked notices began to appear on walls: 'Start the Second Front NOW!' scrawled by impatient individuals. And, sure enough, on June 6th seven hundred ships and more than four thousand landing craft made the famous D-Day landings and once again our hearts were in our mouths as we listened constantly to the wireless and scoured the papers for news. We couldn't bear the thought of another Dunkirk, but knew that was unlikely, as the circumstances were vastly different, and this time our forces were augmented by thousands of American troops. But there would inevitably be further loss of life and more families bereaved. We waited daily for news.

My attention was directed elsewhere the following month, as in July the School Certificate examination took place, and we were kept busy for a couple of weeks, going to different venues for the various subjects we had elected to take. I had chosen eight, one of which had to be Maths, which I dreaded. The others were French, Latin, Art, Biology, English Language, English Literature and Geography (which I hated, but was talked into by Miss Absolom, our form mistress, who taught it.) Eight subjects, looked at today, seem a vast number, but it was not so very unusual then. What a lot of revision there must have been – fortunately any memory of that has receded into oblivion. I worked my way through all these different exams, loving some and hating others. Maths wasn't quite as bad as I expected, but geography – I'll say no more about that. I can't remember *why* it was so boring, but it was.

It was decided that my mother, Olga and I should have a holiday after my exams – the first one since 1939, and we chose to spend a week in Paignton. Emergency ration cards had to be obtained at the Food Office, and we rattled down to Devon in a shabby old train, to stay at a modest guest house near the sea. It was very pleasant to get away from everything, and I resolved not to think about exam results at all. The weather was hot and sunny and we were able to spend much of the time on the beach doing the things we loved and trying not to think about the war. This was not entirely possible. It was a little sad for us to see a number of RAF boys about in the town, for they were staioned nearby, and doing their initial training, as Paul had done in Hastings. I was nearly seventeen, and one day on the way to the beach, was wearing a brief sundress, scarlet with white polka dots, that my mother had made. A group of RAF boys gave me an admiring whistle, and some of them started singing, *"Lady in red – as fresh as a daisy when the town is in bed!"* – a popular song of the moment. I probably blushed at the time, (girls were rather less sophisticated then) but was quite flattered.

Our short holiday proved very beneficial to us all, and helped us to cope with things back home. My exam results arrived, and I was gratified to hear that I had achieved matriculation standard, with three distinctions, (French, Latin and Art), four credits (one in maths, as required) and a pass (geography!). That was a relief, at least, though what I was going to do with my life was still undecided. Everything seemed to be on hold, careers in limbo, future plans impossible to make. But there was a gradual realisation that we were teetering on the edge of victory, and then – surely – we would all be able to see our way forward.

I was determined to leave school after matriculating, though everyone implored me to stay on and take the Higher School Certificate exam. I just couldn't bear the thought of remaining there most of my friends were leaving, so after much argument and pleading I was allowed to do what I wanted. I had no idea in which direction my life was going, so as I was interested in art, and fairly good at it, I went on to Leamington Art School with a view to becoming a commercial artist. That was quite an enjoyable time, and I learned perspective, the effect of reflected light, form shadow and cast shadow, and also a few other things which had very little to do with art! I spent a year there before realising that my career lay in quite another direction.

By this time I was going to dances, at the Blue Café, the Town Hall on a Friday night, and occasionally the Palais, though the latter was considered rather 'common' by my mother. I realise now how much music meant to us then. Our 'pop' music consisted of the wonderful sound of a 'big band' playing all the great hits of that time, especially those of the legendary Glenn Miller – 'Moonlight Serenade', 'Take the 'A' Train', 'Chatanooga Choo-choo', 'In the Mood' and so many others – fabulous to dance to, or just to listen to. Every dance hall had its band, and many cafés their small ensembles – there was so much live music about, and many good singers – or 'crooners', as they were known then. They could actually *sing,* too – and you could hear the words, many of which were worth worth listening to. Vera Lynn of course was queen of them all, with those unforgettable songs she made her own – 'We'll Meet Again', 'White Cliffs of Dover', 'Yours', and so many more. She didn't have the greatest voice, but its special quality went straight to your heart. She wasn't called the 'Forces' Sweetheart' for nothing.

Going to dances meant nice things to wear – or should have done. We had to make do with whatever we could manage from our supply of clothing coupons. Low waisted dresses were all the rage, with a pleated skirt which would swing out when you were jiving. Though clothing was still strictly controlled, and would be for a long time, garments were beginning to be a little less austere and pleats were appearing again. Most of us had one dress like that, but only one, (mine was bought second-hand from June's aunt for three pounds – it was quite a superior model) for we had to remember what other clothes we might need for the colder weather and eke out our coupons accordingly. Blouses and skirts were mixed and matched in an attempt to vary our wardrobes, but it was very difficult. Hair was worn piled up at the front and longish at the back, and unless you had naturally curly hair, 'perms' were essential. And what perms they were! I remember my hair being dowsed in some evil-smelling solution, wound on to tight curlers and wired up to a machine, which was then switched on. You would 'cook' for a prescribed length of time, then the curlers were unwound, and the curls soaked in a neutraliser. Next a shampoo, some strong green setting lotion, a head full of tight pin-curls, and under the drier for goodness knows how long The result of this amazing process depended on the skill of the hairdresser, but you usually came out of the shop with tight sculptured waves and curls. I brushed mine like mad as soon as I got home, and actually I had some very nice, natural-looking perms, but just occasionally the hair would go terribly frizzy and you were stuck with that until it grew out. My first perm cost ten and sixpence (fifty-two and a half pence) and I was very pleased with it. So with our pleated dresses, permed hair and suntan-lotioned legs with a seam drawn up the back to imitate stockings, we were all set for a night out at the Blue Café! Nylons were very new in this country in those days, and hardly ever available in the shops – besides, they were extremely fragile, cost coupons, and might possibly ladder the first time you wore them – hence the made-up legs. They were very highly valued, and a repair service was set up in some dry cleaners, where laddered nylons could be mended. But they were so very scarce, unless you were 'friendly' with a GI, when they would be readily available! Consequently, any girl with luxurious nylon-clad legs was viewed with the deepest suspicion.

There were always young men to dance with, often servicemen home on leave, or boys too young for military service, but there was also another category – young farmers – whose vital work providing much needed food secured them exemption from the forces. June and I became very friendly with some of these, and even joined the Young Farmers' Club, though we had nothing whatever to do with agriculture! It was worth sitting through boring meetings, or demonstrations of how to pluck, draw and truss a chicken, (not that we ever lucky enough to have one) or some such, in order to enjoy the social life which invariably followed. The young farmers were a good crowd, and all had cars, for which they had a special petrol allowance, so there were some enjoyable times to be had at dances in neighbouring villages. Some of them would always turn up at the Blue Café, fairly late in the proceedings, as more often than not they had been busy on the combine harvester until dusk. They certainly avoided combat, but how they worked – and played! It's a good thing that there were so few cars on the road, as a great deal of beer was consumed – (it is to be hoped that it was a relatively weak wartime brew) – and I suspect the standard of driving sometimes left much to be desired. Looking back, I now realise how dangerous it must have been, tearing round the bends in those narrow country lanes with screened headlights, and in cars that had seen better days – no MOTs, spare parts and tyres almost impossible to obtain, and a minimum of maintenance. We must have had a guardian angel keeping his eye on us.

As 1944 drew to a close, a new and different feeling pervaded the country. We waited, shabby, tired, afraid to hope too much, yet gaining confidence that the New Year would bring the news we were all longing for. The British people, after so much suffering, were – tentatively – poised on the threshold of Victory.

THE END OF THE ROAD

By the beginning of 1945 victory was in the air. The Allies were doing well on all fronts and it really did seem that the end of the war was in sight. On January 27th there was heart-breaking news – the Americans had liberated one of Hitler's unspeakable concentration camps – Auschwitz – and discovered thousands of starving and emaciated people, mostly Jewish, who had suffered unimaginable horrors, and many had died, of hunger, disease, or were murdered in the gas chambers. Pictures in the papers were so appalling it was hard to look at them. Our loathing for the Nazis increased – if that were possible. On February 14th 'Bomber' Harris ordered the 'carpet bombing' of Dresden, which virtually destroyed the beautiful old city and killed thousands. It was a terrible thing to do, but at that time we were so incensed with Hitler and the evils of his regime that we felt little emotion. In April two more concentration camps were discovered and liberated – Bergen-Belsen and Dachau – containing similar tragic crowds of starving people and countless emaciated bodies. Our anger was indescribable.

It was a great sorrow to everyone that President Roosevelt did not live to see the imminent victory in which he played such a part, for he died on April 12th, to be succeeded by Harry S Truman. But on April 30th we were greeted by the staggering news that Hitler had committed suicide in his Berlin bunker, together with Eva Braun, whom he had just married. We were speechless – of course we were glad to see the end of him, but most of us wanted to have a hand in his departure from this world, and give him a good send-off. Suicide, we thought, was too painless a way out after the unspeakable crimes he had committed.

The atmosphere of impending victory was electric. I walked down the Parade and saw that there was a long queue at Woodward's department store. "What are they selling?" I asked one of the women who were waiting. "Oh, a lot of red, white and blue bunting, for victory celebrations," she replied, "I believe it's quite cheap." And it was. The government was making sure that we would have the means to celebrate after the long ordeal. People were crowding into the shop to buy the bunting, so I waited with all the others and bought a few yards of each colour. I sat at my mother's old Singer sewing machine and ran up a really outrageous red white and blue dress to wear when the announcement of the end of hostilities was made. Excitement was in the air, and we all talked about current events, and how we would celebrate. Everyone was ransacking their attics for old flags, and anything that was red, white and blue. Some had kept their decorations from the Coronation of 1937, and out they all came to celebrate the coming victory, whether they were suitable or not. A few folk were putting them up already, and strings of slightly frayed flags and faded union jacks were appearing everywhere. Arrangements for street parties were being hurriedly worked out, and scarce rations pooled in an attempt to provide some sort of festive fare for the children. Living on a main thoroughfare like the Parade, we could hardly have a street party, and in any case – inevitably, like those of many other folk, our own family rejoicings were very low key. But when the time came, I walked down the Parade with June in my patriotic dress, and got quite a lot of appreciation, plenty of laughs and a number of approving whistles.

Sure enough, on May 7th Hitler's successor, Admiral Doenitz, signed the document confirming Germany's unconditional surrender. On the same day Churchill stood on the balcony of the Ministry of Health in London and made a speech which warmed our hearts. How I wish I could have been there in the crowd, watching him and soaking up that incredible atmosphere. But we had to make do with the wireless, and were still fired by what he had to say and how he said it:

"This is your victory-" he began, in that unforgettable voice, but he got no farther, as the crowd interrupted with a great shout: *"No! It's YOURS!"*

And it was some time before he was able to resume, for the shouting and cheering was so great. *"It is the victory of the cause of freedom in every land. In all our long history we have never seen a greater day than this. Everyone, man or woman, has done their best. Everyone has tried. Neither the long years, nor the dangers, nor the fierce attacks of the enemy, have in any way weakened the unbending resolve of the British nation. God bless you all."*

The response to this was overwhelming. All the pent-up feelings of our long-beleaguered people were released in a tumult of cheering and shouting. It was one of the greatest moments I can ever remember. At last the war in Europe was at an end. The next day, May 8th, was proclaimed a holiday, and became known as 'VE Day'. At home we were silent. I saw the slow tears running down my mother's face, and knew just what she was thinking. Servicemen would be coming home to their loved ones, but there would be nobody coming home to us. Many, many families were in the same position. I, too, was devastated at the thought, but at my age I couldn't help being cheered by all the rejoicing and the general feeling that a mighty weight had been lifted from our shoulders, though the heaviness which lingered in my heart would remain for years to come.

I went out on to the balcony and looked down the Parade at the brave strings of bunting flapping in the wind, interspersed with union flags, bright and hopeful against the shabby, unpainted buildings. Well, the war in Europe's over, I thought. But at what a cost. So many young lives lost, families like ours devastated, homes destroyed. Could this terrible, broken world ever return to normality? Had all the terrible sacrifice been worth it? At seventeen, I honestly couldn't tell.

Now, reluctantly, and with hindsight, I believe that it was.

EPILOGUE

I stood in the garden the other day as the Red Arrows roared overhead on their way to an air show. All those years ago I had stood in another garden, looking up at the sky in just the same way. But then it was to watch Spitfires and Hurricanes scribbling intricate white vapour trails on the blue summer sky as they grappled with the overwhelming numbers of enemy aircraft.

The deafening noise of the Arrows faded as abruptly as it had begun. In the silence which followed, I caught for a split second the unmistakable note of a Merlin engine.

Cynthia Morey Oxfordshire 2009

Printed in the United Kingdom by
Lightning Source UK Ltd., Milton Keynes
142237UK00001B/26/P